Why You Lose at Chess

by
Fred Reinfeld

21st Century Edition

Fred Reinfeld Chess Classics
Peter Kurzdorfer, General Editor

2016
Russell Enterprises, Inc.
Milford, CT USA

Why You Lose at Chess
by Fred Reinfeld

Fred Reinfeld Chess Classics
Peter Kurzdorfer, General Editor

ISBN: 978-1-941270-26-4 (print)
ISBN: 978-1-941270-27-1 (eBook)

Published by:
Russell Enterprises, Inc.
P.O. Box 3131
Milford, CT 06460 USA

http://www.russell-enterprises.com
info@russell-enterprises.com

Editing and proofreading by Peter Kurzdorfer
Cover by Janel Lowrance

Printed in the United States of America

Table of Contents

Attacker's local superiority
Defender's pawn weaknesses
When not to attack
When to defend

From the Editor

Mid twentieth century best-selling author Fred Reinfeld introduced thousands of players to the wonderful game of chess through his tireless efforts. His books were ubiquitous and covered every conceivable aspect of the royal game.

I was one of countless chess players representing several generations who grew up surrounded by Reinfeld books. We couldn't get enough of them! He not only taught us how to play the game well, but also implanted in us his enthusiastic passion for learning the game.

Fred's books are peppered throughout with words and phrases in italics to emphasize ideas. Moves are punctuated with single, double, and even triple exclamation marks and question marks to span the entire spectrum of emotions the moves conjure up.

He had a way of reducing the most intricate, complicated combinations to their basic components. After Reinfeld explains a combination, it makes sense.

Thus I am pleased and honored to be a part of bringing back my old mentor to new generations of chess players. Russell Enterprises Inc. is engaged in a project of resurrecting the immortal Reinfeld classics, republishing them with the modern algebraic notation in place of the archaic English descriptive notation that was popular years ago to make them accessible to twenty-first century chess players.

This undertaking, begun under General Editor Bruce Alberston, has been passed on to me. So I get to reread these wonderful old books, change the notation in ChessBase, type up Fred's snappy prose, and look out for potential errors.

The few analytical errors that crop up from time to time are easily checked with the monster chess engine Fritz, which Fred never had access to. In those far-off pre-computer days, you analyzed each and every position, including any variations you thought up, with nothing more than a board and pieces, using your knowledge of the pieces' potential.

Thus the few errors are no reflection on the author's ability or knowledge at all. I have called attention to only the most egregious ones, and they certainly do not detract at all from the fresh charm he imparts on each and every position he looks at. The few editing comments are indicated by an asterisk in the text, referring the reader to Notes from the Editor, page 128.

Why You Lose at Chess is vintage Reinfeld. He pulls no punches, showing the reader why he or she loses chess games. This is quite a remarkable feat when you think about it, because he never saw any of the games the vast majority of his readers played. But Fred knew the thinking that lurks behind poor chess decisions, and he let us all know what is wrong or irrelevant or misguided about the types of moves he witnessed far too often.

Beginning with a chapter on self-appraisal, he links a lack of understanding of your own personality with erroneous choices of moves and plans in a chess game. He goes on to delve into playing blindly (with no idea what you are actually doing) or by rote (memorization vs. understanding).

A couple of technical mistakes he points out include a lack of understanding of the tremendous importance controlling the center makes as well as knowing what features in a position should be present in order for an attack to be likely to work.

Among other observations, he gets on amateur players for being easily bored, impatient, lazy, and stubborn. And all of this comes with lucid examples from master play that back up his contentions.

All in all, this is a very excellent treatment of a subject players generally do not pay enough attention to. It has the potential to open anyone's eyes to what playing strong chess can be like by showing what happens to those who fail to do so.

Peter Kurzdorfer
July 2016

Chapter 1

You Have No Idea What Kind of Chess Player You Are

If, as someone has said, tact is "the ability to describe others as they see themselves," then you will find this a tactless book. For I shall describe your chess not as *you* see it, but as *I* see it.

You lose at chess, and you're troubled by your losses.

You've been playing chess for quite a while. You've made some progress – not much. You've given the game some study – not a great deal, to be sure, but then you have neither the time nor the desire to make chess a chore.

For one thing, you may have found chess books disappointing. If you have, it's not entirely your fault. Some chess masters write as if they were addressing a convention of grandmasters somewhere on Mount Olympus.

I've often chuckled, and perhaps you have too, at the title of Capablanca's *Chess Fundamentals* – a book about "fundamentals" that doesn't even bother to tell you how the pieces move or how their moves are recorded. After all, what can you expect from a genius who learned the game at the age of four by watching his father play – and criticized his parent's inept moves even then!

On the other hand, you may have noticed that many a student is too literal-minded to follow abstract discussion of ideas. Years ago a friend

of mine read Znosko-Borovsky's classic, *The Middle Game in Chess* – a book bristling with brilliant insights and original notions. But all my friend got out of the book was an obsession with a maneuver he learned from a brief fragment of a game between Emanuel Lasker and Capablanca.

Here is the position that so impressed him:

Dr. Lasker – Capablanca
World Championship Match, 1921

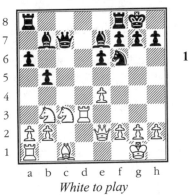

White to play

White is behind in development, and some of his developed pieces are poorly placed. Znosko-Borovsky used this position to demonstrate how cleverly Lasker improved his game and neutralized any bad effects that might have resulted from his poor development.

The Play was:

1.e5 ♘d5 2.♖g3

White threatens ♗h6, winning the exchange, as Black would have nothing better than ...g6 in reply.

2...♘×c3 3.♖×c3 ♕d7 4.♖g3

White renews the threat of ♗h6 etc.

4...♖fd8

Capablanca parries the threat.

5.♗h6 g6

Now Lasker has caught up in development and is not too badly off. Znosko-Borovsky illumines this sequence with an analysis of the play that is really enchanting. But what fascinated my friend was the idea of playing ♖d1 followed by ♖d3 and ♖g3. Ever since he read that book, back in 1923, he has been moving a rook to the third rank in the quixotic hope of winning the exchange by ♖g3. Sometimes he succeeds; other times his peripatetic rook is trapped like a dog.

When he loses the exchange (which happens more often than not), I think regretfully that a little knowledge is a dangerous thing. And when he occasionally wins the exchange, I murmur to myself, "Ah, well, he learned something, even though he did miss 99 percent of what the book had to offer."

So there you have it: it may be your fault, or it may be the author's fault, but in any event studying hasn't helped you much. Let's come back, then, to the ominous question, *why do you lose at chess?* The reasons are many. Let's explore a few of them.

You lose because you have certain misconceptions about your play

So long as these illusions persist, you will not only lose at chess, you will continue to lose at chess. You may make some slight progress, or none at all. On the other hand, discard your current misconceptions and you will strengthen your game appreciably – *even if you never open another chess book for the rest of your life.*

Know yourself – and your opponent

One of your greatest misconceptions is that you view chess as an elaborate kind of solitaire. If only you would realize it, your opponent has just as much a share in the game as you have, with ambitions, strong points, weaknesses, and foibles very similar to your own.

The chess player doesn't live who takes a loss lightly. Have you ever noticed the manner in which chess players resign? Hans Kmoch and I once surveyed these methods in an article called "Unconventional Surrender." We recalled that Alekhine, who was unequaled as a desperate fighter in disheartening situations, occasionally resigned by picking up his king and hurling it across the room. He was a staunch believer in Tartakower's deadpan formula: "Nobody ever won a game by resigning." An admirable principle, but Alekhine rather overdid it.

Then there was Nimzovich, a highly nervous individual and a past master of the bizarre. On at least one occasion he jumped up on a table and screamed, "Why must I lose to this idiot?"

Others, to be sure, were more sedate. Spielmann, that great master of attack about whom you will hear more later, made a face as if he had just swallowed a poisoned bonbon. Rubinstein, indescribably graceful in his chess but hopelessly inarticulate in his social contacts, gave up the ghost with a poker-face expression. As for Grünfeld, that colorless Viennese adding machine of memorized opening variations, he would peevishly stop his clock and steal away silently like an Arab into the night.

Do you know the most famous resignation of all? It happened in this position:

Steinitz – Von Bardeleben
Hastings, 1895

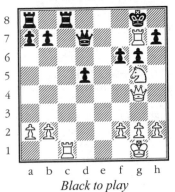

Black to play

Steinitz was 60 years old when this game was played. He had lost his world championship title the year before after a reign of 28 years. Considering his age and physical condition, his play in this game can only be called miraculous.

Now look at Diagram 2. Black is a piece down, but every one of White's pieces is *en prise*, and what is more, Black is threatening mate.

However – and it is a sizable "however" – *Black is in check!* And so formidable is this check that Bardeleben did not have the grace to resign like a man and

congratulate his aged opponent on his magnificent play. Instead, Bardeleben left the playing room and let his time run out on the clock. As soon as that happened, Steinitz reeled off the following forced win:

1...♔h8

If 1...♛×g7 2.♖×c8+ leaves White a clear piece ahead.

On 1...♔×g7 White is able to capture the black queen with *check*.

And in the event of 1...♔f8 White wins with 2.♘×h7+, forcing 2...♔×g7 so that 3.♛×d7+ becomes feasible.

2.♖×h7+! ♔g8

On 2...♛×h7 White plays 3.♖×c8+ etc. (but not 3.♘×h7??? allowing 3...♖×c1+ followed by mate).

**3.♖g7+! ♔h8 4.♛h4+! ♔×g7
5.♛h7+ ♔f8**

Black's moves are all forced.

**6.♛h8+ ♔e7 7.♛g7+ ♔e8 8.♛g8+
♔e7 9.♛f7+ ♔d8 10.♛f8+ ♛e8
11.♘f7+ ♔d7 12.♛d6#!**

We all have our special ways of resigning – not so special, I hope, as Bardeleben's way – but there is no disguising it; it is an unhappy occasion. We feel defeat deeply because chess is one of the most cruelly competitive of all games. The players start off on even terms. The game has so many logical and mathematical features, so many possibilities of exact calculation, that if you lose you are simply crushed. Defeat puts you in such a bad light – or so you think – that, *like all other chess players*, you dread losing. This adds to the other tensions aroused by the game.

(Actually, as you will see in this chapter and later ones, chance, luck, and the clash of personalities play a much greater role in chess than you realize.)

Given these tensions, you need an insight into your own temperament and character, your likes and dislikes, your strong and weak points. If you already possess this insight, you're a very rare chess player indeed. Even world champions fool themselves on occasion and pay a heavy price for their lack of self-knowledge.

A magnificent attacking player fancies himself a careful, conservative master of the golden mean of discretion. An incorrigibly stodgy player, on the other hand, pictures himself as a dashing master of attack. Sometimes these self-deceptions can be charming and amusing. More often they lead to failure and tragedy. They can enfeeble your judgment, rob your game of incisiveness, and cause you to lose faith in your ability.

As you've seen, even a world champion may suffer from this failing. Alexander Alekhine was undoubtedly the greatest chess player in the history of the game, but what he really prided himself on was his...bridge playing! All I know about bridge is that it's played with a deck of cards – or maybe two decks (it's very confusing) – but people in a position to judge have told me that Alekhine was a miserable bridge player. I can well believe it. Just as we misjudge our strong points, so we misjudge our weaknesses.

Since we'll be discussing these strong and weak points, this may be a good place to pause for a little quiz you can ponder as you progress:

Chess personality quiz

(1) Are you energetic and enterprising? Or are you careful and conservative?

(2) Do you like to take chances? Or do you like to play it safe?

(3) Are you bowled over by surprises? Or do you take them in stride?

(4) Does the unfamiliar make you uneasy? Or do you proceed with self-confidence?

(5) Do you tend to overestimate your own skill and underestimate that of your opponents? Or do you tend to underestimate your own skill and overestimate that of your opponents?

(6) Do you like to calculate every detail? Or do you play on impulse?

(7) Are you a slow player? Or a fast player?

Think over these questions carefully and answer them truthfully. Only then will you get the most out of this book.

You may think some of the questions are loaded. You're right. They're worded in such a way that if you can answer them honestly you'll learn a great deal about your chess that you never realized before. Remember this: Self-knowledge is the beginning of wisdom.

Discard your alibi

What's your alibi for losing? You must have one; all chess players have some standard excuse.

Seems even the greatest of masters needs an alibi, so you're in distinguished company. One of our leading American players – let's call him Smith – always wins a high place in the United States Championship Tournament. Smith enters with the expressed hope of winning, but he never does.

When he fails he points out he was in poor physical shape; he'd been working too hard; he'd had little rest and training before the long grind got underway.

A stranger hearing his tale of woe for the first time might inquire, "Well, why didn't you go to the country for a few days? Why didn't you rest? Why didn't you do some training?"

But such questions would be naïve. The alibi is more important than the fact. Indeed, *the alibi creates the fact*. The alibi, in this case and in all cases, has become part of the player's personality; part of his chess; part of his life. He offers the alibi for the first time *after* his first failure. From then on, the alibi exists, ready-made, to be applied unconsciously *before* each subsequent failure.

By invoking his alibi, Smith shields himself from the consequences of his anticipated failure. He also neglects any constructive steps to overcome that anticipated failure. *The alibi is protective. It is also destructive.*

In your own case, your alibi prevents you from improving your game. It prevents you from finding out why you lose at chess.

Not so long ago a player was doing very badly in one of the Hastings Christmas tournaments. Someone asked him sympathetically what the trouble was. He replied, "The other players are too good for me!" Such artless simplicity was disconcerting: it was probably interpreted as sarcasm. For a chess player and his alibi are not soon parted.

One player mutters, "It was my off-day." Another: "I had an easy win, but I muffed it," A third tells you he's out of form. Others have headaches, backaches, upset stomachs, sore throats,

racking coughs. Still others find the light was bad – or too bright. No wonder the great English master Amos Burn ironically remarked that he had never won a game from a well man.

An outstanding player once ascribed his poor showing in a tournament to the fact that he was used to noisy surroundings, while this particular tournament had been played in a quiet locale. The immortal Tarrasch glibly explained that his disappointing Hastings Tournament in 1895 was caused by the sea air. He didn't explain why his successful rivals found the sea air invigorating.

Tarrasch's alibi led to one of the most fantastic stories in the history of tournament play. It came about in this position:

Tarrasch – Teichmann
Hastings, 1895

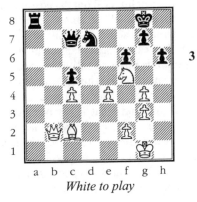

3

White to play

Despite the fact that Tarrasch had to make four moves in two minutes, he fell asleep! "You must move, Doctor!" No answer. (I wish I could say that Teichmann was answered with a snore, but this story is good enough without embroidery.) Again Teichmann called out, and again there was no answer. Finally, on the third call, Tarrasch woke up, looked around wildly, and played

11

1.♘e3 in a flash. But it was too late: he had overstepped the time limit.

There are two ways to take this story. One is to look at Diagram 3. Clearly White has a lost game, as Black's advantage of the exchange is too much for him. Thus:

1.♘e3 ♘e5 2.♘d5 ♛b8

Now, if White exchanges queens, Black's rook reaches b2, which is the beginning of the end.

If White avoids the exchange of queens, Black's queen and rook penetrate along the two open files on the queen's wing. Meanwhile, White's g4-pawn is weak and his bishop has no scope, being hemmed in by its own pawns. No doubt of it: White has a lost game.

But you can forget about the position on the board and think about Tarrasch's extraordinary action. Psychiatrists speak of a state called "narcolepsy," in which a person is prone to fall asleep readily and frequently when he has troubles that are too much for him. Tarrasch would have you believe that he lost because he fell asleep; *what really happened was that he fell asleep because he was lost.* This is a good example of the way rigorous chess analysis gets tangled up with personal reactions.

Tarrasch's opponent in this game, Richard Teichmann, had a strange career. He was nicknamed Richard the Fifth because he generally won the fifth prize in tournaments. He might easily have done better, as we can see from his splendid first prize at Carlsbad in 1911, one of the strongest international tournaments ever held.

When you play over Teichmann's games, you find that they are solid, not to say stolid. You soon get the impression that if Teichmann had put forth more effort he could have been one of the really great ones in chess. Take his extraordinary play in the following weird position:

Teichmann – Amateur
Zürich 1921

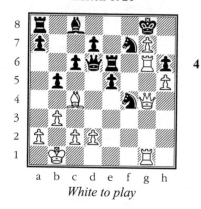

White to play

Teichmann gave the odds of a knight to begin with, and he has since parted with another piece. Now his bishop is attacked and also one of his rooks. To you and me this position would seem absolutely barren of possibilities. But Teichmann sees a tiny ray of hope in the far-advanced g-pawn. Therefore he plays:

1.♖×h6!!

This threatens checkmate beginning with 2.♖h8+!. So Black takes. Why not?

1...♘×h6

If 1...♖×h6 2.♗×f7+! forces mate.

2.♛g5! ♘f7

And now if 2...b×c4 3.♛d8+ decides.

3.♛d8+!! ♘×d8

And now after the queen sacrifice comes a move a surpassing beauty:

4.h6! Resigns!

After 4...b×c4 Black is a queen, rook, and three minor pieces ahead. Yet 5.h7+ forces his resignation. Black is powerless against this threat, as his rook at e6 is pinned.

Few things have been more tragic in chess than the comparative failure of this great master. With such sublime imaginative powers Teichmann nevertheless could not reach the top. His alibi? "Laziness!" For decades that was his trademark.

But the world of master chess has seen even stranger alibis. David Janowsky, a famous contemporary of Tarrasch and Teichmann during the period 1890-1920, was noted for his devil-may-care daring. Here is a position typical of his dashing style:

Janowsky – Schallopp
Nuremberg, 1896

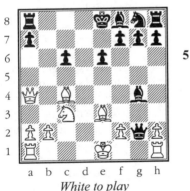

White to play

White is considerably ahead in development. This enables him to peruse his attack and at the same time protect his attacked rook.

Janowsky's move is startling, elegant, and forceful:

1.♗d5!! e×d5

The saucy bishop must be captured, and this is the only way to do it.

2.♕×c6+ ♔d8

If 2...♔e7 3.♘×d5+ forces Black's king back anyway.

3.♕×a8+ ♔d7 4.♕b7+ ♔e6 5.♕c6+ ♗d6 6.♗f4! Resigns

A lovely finish. If 6...♕×h1+ 7.♔d2 ♕×a1 8.♕×d6+ and White mates in two more moves.

From this you can see Janowsky was a Goliath when it came to disposing of second-rate opponents. When Janowsky was matched with really formidable players, however, the story was often a different one. He would play well, get a won game. Then he would begin to procrastinate – to involve himself in needless complications. Take this position from a game he played against Emanuel Lasker:

Dr. Lasker – Janowsky
World Championship Match,1910

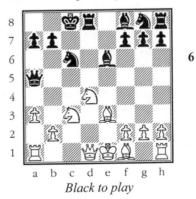

Black to play

Janowsky has a fairly easy win by playing the most obvious move: 1...♗c5. Black then threatens to win a piece. White has no choice; he must try 2.b4.

In that case Black plays 2...♗×d4!.

Now White has two possibilities. One is 3.♗×d4 ♕g5 4.♘b5 a6 and White wins a piece. (4.♘e2 instead leads to an intolerable cramped position for White.)

The other possibility is 3.b×a5 ♗×c3+ 4.♗d2 ♖×d2 and White is lost: 5.♕×d2 ♗×d2+ 6.♔×d2 ♘×a5. Black has two pieces and a pawn for a rook.

But Janowsky has to be fancy. So:

1...♘h6? 2.b4 ♕e5 3.♘cb5

Lasker fights as best he can. (His rival, Tarrasch, once paid him this rather reluctant tribute: "Lasker loses a game now and then, but he never loses his head!")

On 3...a6 Lasker plans 4.♕c1!? a×b5 5.♘×c6 with a counterattack of sorts.

3...♘f5 4.♖c1!

Counterplay on the open file. By pinning Black's knight, he confuses Janowsky and eventually paralyzes his will to win.

4...♘×e3 5.f×e3 ♕×e3+ 6.♗e2 ♗e7 7.♖c3!?

Lasker plays with commendable coolness in a dangerously precarious situation.

He now offers Janowsky the chance of playing 7...♕×c3+! 8.♘×c3 ♘×d4

leaving Black with a very strong game. But once more Janowsky – the dashing Janowsky – falters. "What's the old fox up to?" he wonders. Bemused and indecisive, he manages to snatch defeat from the jaws of victory.

7...♗h4+? 8.g3 ♕e4 9.0-0! ♗f6

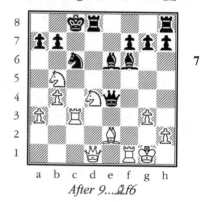

After 9...♗f6

Black's position still looks menacing, but watch how Lasker smashes it.

10.♖×f6!

Removing his worst enemy. The full strength of this move will only become apparent *ten* moves later!

10...g×f6 11.♗f3

At last, after an incredibly patient defense that few players could have conducted, Lasker seizes the initiative. Now there is no dawdling; each move is a hammer blow, stern punishment for Black's indecision.

11...♕e5 12.♘×a7+ ♔c7 13.♘a×c6 b×c6 14.♖×c6+ ♔b8

Now White's king is snug, while Black's is exposed.

**15.♖b6+ ♔c8 16.♕c1+ ♔d7
17.♘xe6 fxe6 18.♖b7+ ♔e8
19.♗c6+ Resigns**

For if 19...♔f8 20.♕h6+ leads to mate.

Just as he did here, so Janowsky missed one decisive line after another, the tournament and match records are strewn with his missed wins. Why? Because "he loved interesting chess"? Because "he was so delighted with a won game he just couldn't bear to part with it"?

Such explanations are poppycock. It's fun to play chess, but it's more fun to win. The real reason Janowsky missed those wins was that he was afraid of the crisis – that awful moment when the fate of the entire game hangs in the balance. Courageous as Janowsky seemed, there must have been a streak of timidity in him that made him shrink from decisions that, once made, can never be called back.

Emanuel Lasker, the world champion from 1894 to 1921, was an altogether different type of player. He was the first to emphasize the *personal* role in chess and to characterize the game as a struggle. He had a clear notion of his own qualifications as well as those of his opponents. Consequently he was able to steer the play into channels wherein his opponents could go astray. When it came to creating complications, this superb fighter spared neither himself nor his opposition.

I like this frank comment Lasker made on his lifetime of hard-fought chess:

"Of my 57 years I have applied at least 30 to forgetting most of what I have learned or read. And once I succeeded in this, I acquired a certain ease and cheer which I should never again like to be without. If need be, I can do that of which I have no idea at present. I have stored little in my memory, but I can apply that little, and it is of use in many and varied emergencies. I keep it in order but resist every attempt to increase its dead weight."

These words admirably convey Lasker's poise, his calm self-confidence, his unsurpassed generalship. When you play over any of his games you see clearly how the personal element reveals itself in chess.

To return to the subject of alibis. How do you suppose Lasker's contemporaries regarded him? Did they praise his marvelous maturity of outlook and his magical ability to handle critical positions? Not exactly. They credited his success not to superlative play but to the rank stogies he smoked.

It's always more convenient to blame your defeat on cigars than on inferior play. And it's much, much easier to invoke your alibi than to try to improve your game. So, instead of saying wistfully, "If only I could play the openings better, everything would be fine," for the love of Caissa, learn them!

Of course, the alibi most often heard is: "He plays too slow! I have a won game against him, and then he drives me nuts with his endless stewing over every move – and bang! there goes the old ball game!"

You've not only heard this one often, you've used it even oftener yourself!

15

For slow play – your opponent's, not your own, of course – is the universal alibi of all chess players.

How much substance is there to it? Not much. Here's why: Both players – you and your opponent – are confusing *time* with *duration*. When it's your move you're so absorbed in your own thoughts that you don't realize how time is passing. Your opponent, on the other hand, is idle and fidgety, waiting impatiently for his turn.

(Buckle, the famous historian, who was also a pretty good chess player, once commented tartly: "The slowness of genius is hard to bear, but the slowness of mediocrity is insufferable!")

Subjectively you feel you've taken very little time for your move, whereas your opponent's irritated impression is that you've taken ages. (He may even go a step further and hint darkly that you're being slow on purpose – a war of nerves.)

But now it's your opponent's move. What happens? The roles are reversed, and this time it's your opponent who has the illusion that he's taking no time at all, while you succumb to the illusion that he's disgracefully slow in making up his mind.

Think it over. I believe you'll agree the picture I've drawn is not exaggerated. What to do about it?

To begin with, overcome your irritation. You're playing chess for fun. If it isn't fun, why play?

But overcoming your irritation is easier said than done. Perhaps this suggestion might help. All the difficulty arises while you're waiting for your opponent to move. But why must you wait idly?

Instead of twiddling your thumbs, *why not put the extra time to good use?* It's yours for free.

For example, check the position to see if any captures, attacks, of threats are available. You'll be pleasantly surprised to find you can get a clearer picture of the situation now that you're momentarily freed from the responsibility of making a decision.

Nor is this all you can do. Why not look at the position from your opponent's point of view? Why not ask yourself what you would do in his place? What would your move be in the immediate situation? What would be your long-range plan?

By spending *his* time in this fashion, you'll not only calm your nerves, you'll also get an insight into the game you've never had before. And, best of all, instead of cultivating a future alibi, you'll be improving your chess in a constructive manner.

Have faith in your play

Self-assurance, or even a reasonable facsimile of same, is a potent weapon in chess. If you're confident of achieving the impossible, you may – believe it or not – succeed in your improbable project. *But if you're doubtful of achieving what is well within your powers, you'll fail in even that limited objective.*

In chess it's wise to understand yourself, of course. But you have to understand the other fellow too. Self-knowledge is hard to come by. Understanding of others is even harder.

As you know, chess players take defeat with considerable bitterness. To protect themselves against disappointment, they invoke standard alibis to sooth their bruised egos. So, often they dread to be put to the test. They go to a chess club, but avoid playing. Some are so self-conscious they imagine everyone's eye is on them, that every onlooker is poised to sneer at each move they make.

To some extent this fear is understandable. We're all afraid of the unknown, and a crucial test before strangers is an ordeal. But you're really punishing yourself without cause; for you may be sure your opponent is just as troubled as you are: your disagreeable experience is not unique.

It may help you to know that even the greatest masters suffer from such feelings of anxiety. Those who exude the most convincing air of self-confidence are usually the most disturbed. Take this account of Najdorf's conduct, which appeared at the conclusion of one of the strongest international tournaments of modern times:

"For all his ingenuity and numerous successes of late, Najdorf has never before scored so impressive a triumph.

"According to Najdorf's own statements, however, he was lost in every game. No sooner had he made a certain number of moves than he would storm into the pressroom – almost with the punctuality of a clock – to announce wildly that he was going to lose because of some oversight, some grave risk, or some surprising move by an opponent.

"Though these dramatic announcements were repeated with all the dramatic intensity of which Najdorf is capable, none ever came through. That dreadful attack of Reshevsky's – it came to a standstill. That careless sacrifice against Gudmundsson – it proved to be sound. That surprise of Pilnik's – it worked as a boomerang.

"Like many of his colleagues past and present, Alekhine included, Najdorf plays really well only if pricked to the utmost alertness by the spur of fear. He is unique, however, in freely admitting so with complete disregard for 'face.' As he commented on one such occasion: 'I just have the urge to undress myself in public.'"

I can give you other examples. The most remarkable one I recall was Capablanca's astounding article in *The New York Times* just before the tournament of 1927. The world champion on the eve of one of the greatest triumphs of his career proclaimed in the bleakest terms that he was very dubious about his prospects.

(Doesn't this remind you of Smith's alibi? It might be classified as "the preliminary and propitiatory Alibi." The next time Capablanca used the alibi was in connection with his loss of the world championship to Alekhine – a loss that surprised himself and everyone else, with the exception of Alekhine!)

The following play will give you some idea of the vast golf between Capablanca's despondent forecast and his superb moves a few days later.

Nimzovich – Capablanca
New York 1927

8

Black to move

Capablanca, who has in mind a very pretty sacrifice of the queen, opens up the position with:

1...e5! 2.♗×e5 ♖dd2

Threatening ...♖×f2 with a mating attack by the powerfully entrenched rooks.

If White defends with 3.♖f1, Black has the crushing continuation 3...♕×e3! and if 4.f×e3 ♖g2+ 5.♔h1 ♖×h2+ 6.♔g1 ♖cg2#.

3.♕b7 ♖×f2 4.g4

Desperately trying to use the bishop to defend the kingside. But Capablanca foils him.

4...♕e6! 5.♗g3 ♖×h2!

Masterly play. If now 6.♗×h2 ♕×g4+ 7.♔h1 ♕h3! forcing checkmate.

6.♕f3 ♖hg2+ 7.♕×g2 ♖×g2+ 8.♔×g2 ♕×g4

Capablanca has an easy win, what with his advantage in material and position. Nimzovich resigned after eight more moves.

How can one reconcile Capablanca's doubts with his superb play and his jaunty air of complete self-confidence during the tournament? This kind of tension before the battle reminds us of the painful stage fright that afflicts even veteran actors and concert artists. Years of experience cannot save them from the agony that overcomes them just before curtain time. Yet, only moments later they display the skill and mastery that have made them outstanding in their profession.

A belief in the "impossible," on the other hand, is one of those vital illusions that can make you a better chess player. Perhaps you know the statement credited to Chigorin, that great Russian master of the eighties and nineties. The story is that when he had White he always played 1.e4, confident that he had the better game. When he had Black he answered 1.e4 with 1...e5, just as firmly convinced that he had at least an even game!

Consider those two statements together, and you will say they are logically ridiculous. Granted. Indeed, there is much in chess that eludes logic, and you will be a better player if you realize it.

As it happens, Chigorin's remark is by no means as fantastic as it sounds; it contains an "inarticulate minor premise" that makes a good deal of sense. What he was really saying was this: "When I, the great Chigorin, have White, then White has the better game.

When I, the great Chigorin, have Black, then Black has at least an equal game!"

To drive home this tricky point, let's look at two delightful games won by Chigorin – the first with the white pieces, the second with the black forces.

In the first game Chigorin defeats an authority on opening play in 15 moves, using an opening which is nowadays seen only in the antique shop:

Chigorin – Gossip
Ponziani Opening
New York 1889

1.e4 e5 2.♘f3 ♘c6 3.c3 d5

A much simpler countermeasure is 3...♘f6 4.d4 d5! with equality.

4.♕a4 f6

Such early advances of the f-pawn can be very damaging.

5.♗b5 ♘ge7 6.e×d5 ♕×d5 7.0-0 ♗d7 8.d4

If Black were a good player, he would now free himself cleverly with 8...e×d4 9.c×d4 ♘e5! 10.♗×d7+ ♕×d7!.

As Black plays, he soon finds himself in serious difficulties which Chigorin exploits to the utmost.

8...e4? 9.♘fd2 ♘g6 10.♗c4 ♕a5 11.♕b3 f5 12.♗f7+

The beginning of the end. Trust Chigorin to dispose of a king surrounded by swarming enemies.

12...♔e7? 13.♘c4 ♕a6 14.♗g5+! ♔×f7

Chigorin finishes the game at once with a drastic double check, theoretically the strongest move known to chess:

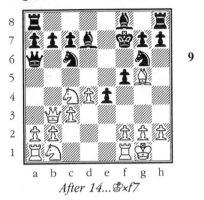

After 14...♔×f7

15.♘d6#

Now comes part two, showing what Chigorin accomplished with the black pieces:

Schlechter – Chigorin
Latvian Gambit
St. Petersburg, 1878

1.e4 e5 2.♘f3 f5 3.e×f5

Now White could play 3.♘×e5, threatening ♕h5+. Black's best is 3...♕f6, but after 4.d4 d6 5.♗c4 f×e4 6.♘c3 White has a notable lead in development.

3...♘c6 4.♗b5 ♗c5! 5.♗×c6 d×c6 6.♘×e5 ♗×f5

Chigorin has developed rapidly, but, as you will see, his last move requires considerable foresight.

7.♕h5+ g6 8.♘×g6?!

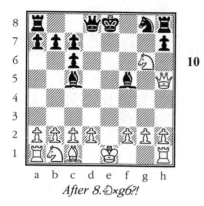

After 8.♘xg6?!

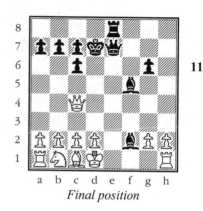

Final position

White is hypnotized by sordid thoughts of material gain. If now 8...♗xg6 (which he expects), then 9.♕xc5 leaves him two pawns ahead.

8...hxg6‼ 9.♕xh8 ♕e7+

Black's three developed pieces now harry White's king to his doom. If 10.♔f1 ♗xc2 and the threat of ...♗d3+ is decisive.

10.♔d1 ♗xf2!

This rules out the interposition f2-f3 and therefore threatens ...♗g4#. True, Chigorin is leaving a piece or two *en prise*, but these matters are too trifling to worry about.

11.♕xg8+ ♔d7

Now if 12.♕xa8 ♗g4#.

12.♕c4 ♖e8! Resigns

White's decision is a wise one in the face of Chigorin's threat: 13...♕e1+! 14.♖xe1 ♖xe1#.

If 13.d3 ♕e2#. Or if 13.d4 ♗g4+ 14.♔d2 ♕e3#.

After playing over these two games, you can see that Chigorin's claim had a logic all its own: the logic of his dazzling skill, which made short work of inferior opponents.

Differentiate among your opponents

So it comes right down to a question of personalities. So much of chess does. This statement may shock you, for you will not find it in any chess book. Yet the masters themselves often discard logic in favor of the personal approach.

Compare the play of a chess master in a tournament with his games in a simultaneous exhibition. Does he produce the same type of chess in both events? Certainly not.

In an exhibition, where he must move quickly against a group of weaker players, the master knows he can get away with moves that would rarely work against another master.

Suppose he is faced with this situation: he can (a) win a pawn with a great deal of simplifying or (b) refuse the pawn in order to maintain a complicated position full of vague but menacing promise. In a game with another master he is likely to take the pawn and welcome the simplification. *However, in a simultaneous exhibition he will probably choose the complicated course.*

Why this difference? For one thing, he is too discreet to toy with a powerful opponent, whereas in dealing with simultaneous players, experience and statistics tell him the defense will collapse in the face of determined and complex attack.

If you've ever played in simultaneous exhibitions you've probably met such conditions yourself. On one side of the board is the able, experienced, self-confident master waiting to pounce on your slightest blunder. And on the other side, you, the amateur, unsure of yourself, bewildered by the position, nagged by a sense of impending disaster.

One of the many facets of Alekhine's genius was his remarkable flair for sensing these difficulties. The following masterpiece brings out the sharp distinctions between master play and simultaneous play:

Alekhine – Mindeno
Ruy Lopez
Simultaneous exhibition, 1933

1.e4 e5 2.♘f3 ♘c6 3.♗b5 d6

Modern masters do not care for this defense, as it leads to a cramped and passive position for Black.

4.d4 e×d4 5.♛×d4

Gaining time for later castling on the queenside.

5...♗d7 6.♗×c6 ♗×c6 7.♘c3 ♘f6 8.♗g5 ♗e7 9.0-0-0 0-0

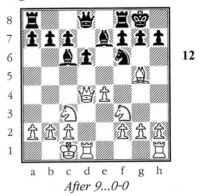

After 9...0-0

White has to make a fateful decision here.

The essentials of the position are as follows: Black's position, as we know, is rather restricted. White can either quietly strengthen his position in the hope of maintaining his grip on the situation or he can create complications in which his threats will panic Black.

A few months earlier, playing against the Danish master Andersen in the International Team Tournament at Folkstone, Alekhine in the identical position selected the first method. That game went 10.♖he1 ♘d7 11.♗×e7 ♛×e7 12.♖e3 ♛f6 (Black's purpose is to try to free himself by simplifying exchanges.)

The game continued: 13.♘d5 ♗×d5 14.e×d5 ♛×d4 15.♘×d4 ♖fe8 16.♖de1 ♖×e3 17.♖×e3. White is left with a microscopic advantage in mobility which was good enough to enable Alekhine to win.

21

But that was a master game. Here's how Alekhine plays against an amateur:

10.h4

A sly move which somehow suggests to Black the suicidal idea of threatening, and then capturing, White's bishop.

10...h6 11.♘d5!

Black can still come out with a whole skin by playing 11...♘xd5! 12.exd5 ♗d7. But the power of suggestion is too much for him.

11...h×g5? 12.♘×e7+ ♕×e7 13.h×g5

After this the open h-file must decide in White's favor, despite his material minus.

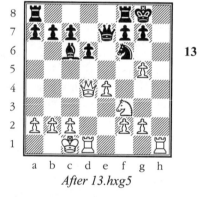

After 13.hxg5

Even the exchange of queens cannot neutralize White's attack. Try this variation: 13...♕xe4 14.gxf6 ♕xd4 15.♖xd4 ♗xf3 16.gxf3. Now 16...gxf6? allows 17.♖g4#! Or if 16...♖fe8 17.♖g4! g6 18.♖gh4 and Black succumbs to ♖h8#.

13...♘×e4 14.♖h5 ♕e6 15.♖dh1 f5

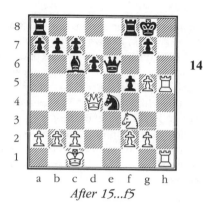

After 15...f5

Though working under a great strain, Black can now afford to be complacent.

True, White has 16.g6 (threatens mate) 16...♕xg6 17.♘e5!?, which seems to win; for if 17...dxe5? 18.♕c4+ and after 18...♕f7 or 18...♖f7 there follows 19.♖h8#.

But here's why Black is laughing in his beard: after 17.♘e5!? he plays 17...♕xh5! 18.♖xh5 dxe5 with more than enough material for his queen.

Can it be that the amateur has out bluffed the master? Not at all. With a pitying smile Alekhine *transposes moves*, picking up his knight and slamming it down triumphantly in a move of pure genius.

16.♘e5!!!

This beautiful move has three subtle points.

The first: if now 16...♕xe5 17.♕xe5 dxe5 18.g6 and Black is helpless against the coming ♖h8#.

Meanwhile, White threatens ♖h8# anyway, so that the knight must be captured.

16...d×e5 17.g6! Resigns

And here's the second point of White's delightful combination: if 17...♕×g6 18.♕c4+ forces mate!

And the third point of the combination? Go back to Diagram 14. If White plays 16.g6 ♕×g6 17.♕c4+ Black has the simple defense 17...d5.

By playing 16.♘e5!!! Alekhine brought about the removal of Black's d-pawn so that the defense ...d6-d5 was ruled out!

You would have to go far to find a more artistic game, and yet the turning point that made it possible for White to win came at moves 10 and 11. White's psychological swindle is the fuse that sets off the explosion.

So there you have the difference between tournament play and simultaneous play. In a game between two masters the odds are against the success of speculative attacks. They might succeed, say, in one game out of ten. In a simultaneous exhibition, the same policy succeeds 999 times out of a thousand.

The Shock Value of Surprise

Even in games between first-class players, an unsound move, if introduced with an element of bluff, has a fighting chance to succeed. I once discovered this in an amusing game I played in the Marshall Chess Club Championship.

My opponent, a strong player, adopted the King's Indian Defense. Soon we came to a semi-blocked position, with heavy maneuvering indicated for both sides. Though my opponent's moves were excellent, he was running into time trouble by playing much too slowly. Eventually he had about two minutes left in which to make 20 moves.

Noting this, I played my king from g1 to f2, then to e3 on successive moves – with almost all the pieces still on the board. My opponent, as I anticipated, stared at the king with glassy eyes as he tried desperately to figure out the rhyme or reason behind my crazy king wanderings.

The king moves were bad – so bad that ♔e3 gave him a chance to win my queen by discovered check. But my gaping opponent saw nothing. He stared at the board as if hypnotized, while the seconds kept ticking away. Soon he lost the game by overstepping the time limit.

Of course this is an extreme case. But it does show the disastrous effects of surprise. Another example I recall involves a different, but far more common, stratagem.

The game I have in mind was played in the Manhattan Chess Club Championship, also against a fairly good player. Toward the beginning of the middlegame I saw a chance for a speculative pawn sacrifice. It looked inviting, and I began to examine its consequences. After a good deal of "if he does this, I'll do thus-and-so," I suddenly thought to myself: "You dope! 'Speculative' means 'speculative,' and if you're going to sac a pawn, sac it and damn the consequences."

No sooner said than done. I made the move incisively and sat back comfortably. My opponent looked startled, then studied me appraisingly, then buckled down to work. Was the move sound or unsound? I could see suspicion struggling with worry and fear. He stared intently at the position, raising his eyebrows now and then to snatch a hurried look at me as if to read the answer to his problem from my expression.

His choice, as you may have guessed, was not too easy. One move enabled him to take the pawn safely, though not without subjecting himself to some annoyance. Another capture would expose him to all sorts of difficulties; while a third method would lose a piece in three forced moves.

Which move did he choose? Before I tell you, I must explain that, although he is a strong player, his forte is clear, simple positions where no risk is involved. He shuns tactics, and when given a choice of two or more possibilities, he becomes hesitant. In the end, after half and hour's study, he chose the wrong capture and soon lost a piece.

The masters, you may be sure, are well aware of this tactic. Some of the more enterprising ones, like Rudolf Spielmann for example, have systematically indulged in unsound sacrifices which had the *look* of being charged with dynamite. Though damned later on by fastidious critics, who had never made a move in anger, he achieved a high percentage of success in his games.

The following shows how a great master successfully springs a surprise on his opponent. The game has been called the most brilliant ever played, and yet no one knows to this day whether it's sound or not!

Alekhine – Böök
Queen's Gambit
Margate 1938

1.d4 d5 2.c4 d×c4 3.♘f3 ♘f6 4.e3 e6 5.♗×c4 c5

The disappearance of Black's d-pawn from the center gives White a free hand in that important zone. A dynamic attacking player like Alekhine does not need an engraved invitation before taking advantage of such a situation.

6.0-0 ♘c6 7.♕e2 a6 8.♘c3 b5 9.♗b3 b4 10.d5!

The attack starts. If 10...e×d5 11.♘×d5! ♘×d5 12.♖d1 and White wins back the piece with a decisive advantage.

10...♘a5 11.♗a4+ ♗d7 12.d×e6 f×e6

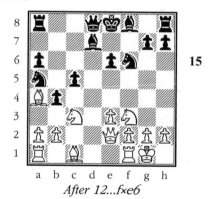

15

After 12...f×e6

In this position Alekhine played one of the most astounding moves ever seen in a game of chess. Instead of salvaging his attacked knight (as you or I would have done), he studied the position for a long time and finally played:

13.♖d1!!? b×c3 14.♖×d7! ♘×d7 15.♘e5 ♖a7 16.b×c3!

Alekhine has sacrificed a rook – for what? For nothing more than to put Black in an uneasy frame of mind.

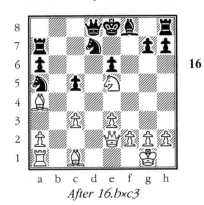

16

After 16.bxc3

16...♔e7?!

Hoping to get rid of the burdensome pressure by freeing himself from the pin.

17.e4!

A devilish move. On 17...♘xe5 White wins by 18.♗g5+.

Black is lost now. Here is the impressive way Alekhine wound up this extraordinary game.

17...♘f6 18.♗g5 ♕c7 19.♗f4 ♕b6 20.♖d1 g6 21.♗g5 ♗g7 22.♘d7!

This murderous blow is the beginning of the end for Black.

22...♖xd7 23.♖xd7+ ♔f8 24.♗xf6 ♗xf6 25.e5! Resigns

If the bishop retreats, White plays 26.♕f3+ with mate to follow.

When the game was over, Spielmann, the great specialist in this type of attack,

reproached the loser: "How can you play like that? Such sacrifices always pay off in over-the-board play!" A hot discussion started over the critical position. That argument is still going on to this day.

Annotators have written pages and pages asserting that White's attack is foolproof. Others just as vociferous claim Black has a perfectly satisfactory defense. To my knowledge no one has yet had the final word.

What, then, is our verdict? Experts, working in the quiet of their studies with unlimited time at their disposal, have been unable to arrive at the truth. Consequently we can agree that Alekhine's inspired "swindle" was well worth trying – especially under the conditions of a time limit.

Alekhine, of course, know he had many factors in his favor. First, his enviable reputation practically assured belief in the soundness of the sacrifice – this on the skimpy but impressive theory that if Alekhine played it, it must be sound.

Furthermore, the intimidating presence of this awe-inspiring personality was enough to befuddle Black. Then, consider the shock effect always registered on the defender by a surprise sacrifice. The more unexpected the sacrifice, the stronger the shock; and *this* sacrifice was altogether out of the ordinary.

Finally, think of the defender's self-doubt: his fear of ridicule if he misses the right defense, his sinking feeling that it is all too late, self-recriminations and reproaches as the minutes tick away. Is it any wonder the defender goes to pieces?

Games like this one go far to explain Spielmann's reliance on sacrifices that lie on the shadowy border between the sound and the unsound. The critic may later sneer at these sacrifices. Nevertheless, in the words of Tarrasch, *"It is not enough to be a good player; you must also play well."*

Even Tarrasch, great player that he was, succumbed more than once to the shock of a surprise onslaught by a keen master tactician. When Lasker made his memorable remark about Tarrasch's "lacking the passion that whips the blood," he was thinking of such games as this one:

Duras – Tarrasch
Ruy Lopez
San Sabastian, 1912

1.e4 e5 2.♘f3 ♘c6 3.♗b5 a6 4.♗a4 ♘f6 5.d3 d6 6.c3 g6

The theorists will tell you that in Lopez variations where White plays the rather conservative d2-d3, Black stands to gain the initiative by eventually advancing ...d6-d5. All very true, but what they fail to tell you is that White is a determined, tricky, and relentless tactician, while his opponent is a rather hidebound theorist who has seen his best days.

7.h3 ♗g7 8.♗e3 0-0 9.♕c1 b5 10.♗c2 ♖e8 11.♗h6 ♗h8 12.♘bd2 d5! 13.♘b3 ♕d6 14.g4 ♘d8!

Having freed his game, Black is now ready for ...♘e6, followed by ...♘f4, or by ...c5 and ...c4, or by ...d4.

15.♕e3! ♘e6!

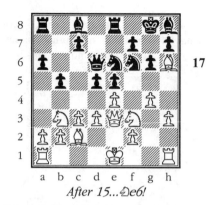

After 15...♘e6!

Black has achieved a splendid game, and Duras knows that only trickery can save him. Here is his surprise:

16.♘×e5!!?

Now, if Black is calm and can assimilate the shock of this astonishing move, he can get the better game with 16...d×e4! 17.d4 c5!.

16...♕×e5?

He thinks Duras has blundered.

17.d4 ♕d6 18.e5 ♕d8

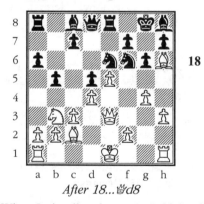

After 18...♕d8

When I visualize the scene I think of Tarrasch as trying hard to conceal a triumphant smile. If White plays 19.e×f6?? then Black plays 19...♘f8 and thus wins the queen.

26

But now comes a second surprise, even more shattering than the first.

19.0-0-0!!

So Duras gives up the piece on spec. He has a lasting pressure in return, as Black can never free himself.

19...♘d7 20.f4! ♗g7 21.♗×g7 ♘×g7 22.f5 ♘f8 23.♖df1

What a pawn-roller! White's threats suggest themselves almost without thought – for example, ♕h6 followed by ♘d2-f3-g5 and f5-f6 in some cases. Black escapes this, only to lose in an equally drastic way.

23...g×f5 24.g×f5 ♕h4 25.♘d2 f6 26.♖hg1! ♖e7 27.♖g4! ♕h5 28.♕f3!

This brutal move leaves Black defenseless, the threats being 29.♖×g7+ winning the queen or 29.♕×d5+ winning a rook or 29.e×f6 winning a piece.

28...♕f7 29.e×f6! ♕×f6 30.♕×d5+ Resigns

White wins a rook to begin with. This game is one of my special favorites because it reveals so dramatically the force of personality in chess.

The Eternal triangle

So far I've indicated some of the ways in which the personal factor dominates a game of chess. Just to clinch the argument, if you're still unconvinced, consider the following enigma: A consistently bests B; B consistently beats C; yet C consistently beats A!

You've probably seen this happening in your club. Very likely it's happened to you.

How can this be explained? Certainly not on the basis of logic or on the comparative strength of the players involved. Use either of these criteria, and the triple relationship becomes utter nonsense. *The explanation must necessarily lie in the realm of personality.*

Let me tell you of one such trio and the strange, illogical bond that held it together. It was made up of Sammy Reshevsky, Reuben Fine, and myself. Though I was not in the same league with these two, I "belonged." Here's why: Reshevsky consistently defeated Fine: Fine consistently beat me; yet I had one of the best records any player ever achieved against Sammy!

My losing most of the time to Fine was no mystery, since he was the better player. Add to this my wholesome respect for his ability; as youngsters we played and studied chess together – even wrote some chess books together instead of doing our homework.

But I now know – many years later – that it wasn't Fine's superior skill that accounted for the completely one-sided result. What really had me licked was the "go-to-hell" expression on his face, the withering arrogance of his attitude toward all opponents. I shouldn't have been intimidated – but I was. I was a beaten man before I started to play.

This brings us to the second riddle. Why didn't Fine's arrogance affect Reshevsky?

Well, for a variety of reasons. To begin with, Sammy has a sublime confidence in himself that dwarfs even Fine's pride. Sammy doesn't get excited about it, you understand. He merely contemplates his own genius with deep respect and serene admiration. He's just as certain he's going to win as he is that the sun wouldn't dare bypass Texas.

Sammy had other advantages. He's much more phlegmatic than Fine and consequently better equipped to handle tense situations. When he runs into positions that would break the heart of another player, he merely fights harder. Naturally this was disconcerting to Fine.

Still another point in Sammy's favor was that he has virtually no interests outside of chess. Fine, on the other hand, has several. Consequently, Fine never commanded the same absorption in the game that was Sammy's for the asking.

For these reasons, if for no other, Fine always proved easy prey for Sammy. If Fine had a lost game, he lost it. If he had a won game, he drew it.

To the best of my recollection, Fine managed to eke out only one win against Reshevsky, and that after years of trying. Who can ever forget their game in the 1940 United States Championship in which Sammy was no near losing that he was in tears? Yet he drew the game and kept the title! Here's the position in which the fate of this game was decided:

Fine – Reshevsky
United States Championship 1940

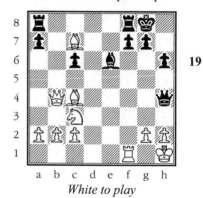

White to play

With two pieces for a rook, White has an easy win. All he has to do is release the pin on his light-square bishop. There is a simple way to do this, and a complicated way. Fine chooses the complicated way – a foolish procedure against a player like Sammy, who has at least nine lives.

The simple way is 1.♖f4 and Black's downfall is certain.

Instead, Fine played:

1.♗f4? ♗×c4 2.♕×c4 g5 3.g3 ♕g4

This is the position Fine wanted, but now, to his dismay, he finds that it won't do! This is why:

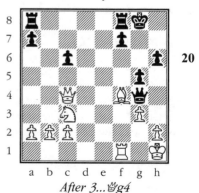

After 3...♕g4

28

His intended move is 4.♞e4, getting rid of the pin and also threatening the baleful knight fork 5.♞f6+. But, as often happens when Sammy is beaten, he has a perfect defense, as follows:

4.♞e4 ♛e6!

If now 5.♛xe6 fxe6 and the bishop, pinned along the file, is lost!

5.♛d4 f5! 6.♞c5 ♛e2

And here if 7.♖g1, Black does not foolishly play 7...gxf4??? allowing 8.gxf4+ and wins. Instead he plays 7...♛f3+ 8.♖g2 ♛f1+ with a draw.

7.♖f2 ♛e1+ 8.♔g2 gxf4

And Black has escaped!

Actually Fine did not play 4.♞e4. In the position of Diagram 20 he continued 4.♛xc6 gxf4 5.♖xf4 ♛e6 6.♛f3 f5 7.♛d5 ♖ae8 8.♔g2 ♛xd5+ 9.♞xd5 with two pawns for the exchange. But Black is out of the woods, and the game eventually ended in a draw.

Now we come to an even greater riddle – Sammy's helplessness against me. In the five tournament games I played him I won the first two and drew the remaining three. Why did I succeed where Fine had failed?

No logical technical reasoning can explain it. The answer lies entirely in my attitude toward Reshevsky. Unlike Fine, I was not his rival. Hence my first feeling in playing Sammy was one of relief rather than fear. It was no disgrace to lose to this great master – that could happen to anyone. I had nothing to lose; I had shed my responsibilities; I was carefree as one rarely is in tournament chess.

What a paradox: I was carefree, and Sammy was never carefree! Chess to Sammy was a very serious business. The combination of these factors was enough to put me in the best of spirits and to release my imagination. I played with great confidence and richness of ideas. And so I made an enviable record against this formidable player, so superior to me in technical skill.

In our very first game I overwhelmed Sammy with three unpleasant surprises:

Reinfeld - Reshevsky
Queen's Indian Defense
Minneapolis (Western Championship)
1932

1.d4 ♞f6 2.c4 e6 3.♞f3 b6 4.g3 ♗b7 5.♗g2 c5? 6.d5!

The first unwelcome surprise for Sammy. By means of this temporary pawn sacrifice I get a powerful pawn center and he is left with a constricted position.

6...exd5 7.♞h4 g6 8.♞c3 h6 9.0-0 a6 10.cxd5 d6 11.e4 ♗g7 12.f4

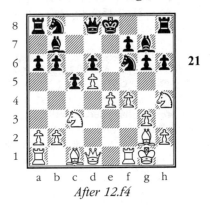

After 12.f4

Black must now guard against e4-e5 which, if it becomes feasible, will destroy his position.

12...♘fd7 13.a4! 0-0 14.♗e3 ♔h7 15.♕c2

Before striving for e4-e5 I strengthen my position and develop more pieces.

15...♘f6 16.h3 ♘bd7 17.♖ae1 ♖e8 18.♗f2 ♘g8

As you see, Sammy has worked hard to prevent e4-e5. *And yet the move is playable!* This is the second surprise, even more unpleasant than the first one:

After 18...♘g8

19.e5!! d×e5 20.f5!!

The point of the breakthrough. If now 20...g5 21.f6+ wins a piece. And if 20...g×f5 21.♘×f5 with the winning threat of 22.♘d6+.

20...♘f8 21.f×g6+ f×g6 22.♗e4 ♕d6 23.♗e3 ♘e7 24.♖f7 ♔g8 25.♖ef1 ♘×d5?!

The pressure has piled on pitilessly, and Black has no good move left. In the event of 25...♘f5 I continue as in the actual play.

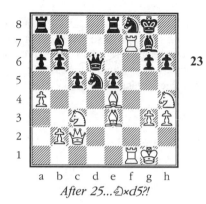

After 25...♘×d5?!

26.♖×b7!

The third surprise: it looks like an oversight – but it isn't.

26...♘×e3 27.♕f2

So that if 27...♘×f1 28.♕f7+ and 29.♕×g7#.

27...♘f5 28.♘×f5

Or 28.♗×f5, winning a piece, for if 28...g×f5 29.♖×g7+! wins (29...♔×g7 30.♘×f5+, forking king and queen).

28...g×f5 29.♕×f5 ♔h8 30.♖f7

Or 30.♕f7 ♘e6 31.♕g6 and wins.

30...♘g6

Here Sammy overstepped the time limit with ten more moves to make before reaching the time control. However, after 31.♕×g6 his resignation would have been in order.

A perfect example of how self-confidence can help you defeat a much better player than yourself! Think it over. You'll find a great deal in this analysis of "the eternal triangle" that applies to you. Know yourself – and you opponent. You'll get more out of chess – more wins. And more fun, too.

Chapter 2

You Play the Openings Blindly or by Rote

If you're so inept a golfer that you get your ball trapped in the rough and have to waste precious strokes to get it out again, all the cussing in the world won't change the fact that you've spoiled your score and ruined your day's pleasure.

If your bidding at bridge leaves you with an impossible contract to fulfill, it's clear that your goose is cooked right then and there.

The same is true of chess. Play the opening badly and you have no prospects in the middlegame; your defeat is likely – perhaps inevitable.

In other games this sequence of cause and effect is clear to most players. But in chess many of us miss the connection. We think of the opening as a *prelude* to the game – not as a *part* of the game, and perhaps the most important part at that. If we're inexperienced we make the opening moves blindly, unknowingly storing up future misery for ourselves. If we've read a book or two we dash through the opening heedlessly, playing the moves by rote, in a hurry to get to the "real" game.

Even masters, who ought to know better, are sometimes guilty of this fault. Not so long ago I read an account of an international match in which one of the masters played his first 14 moves in three minutes. He resigned nine moves and several minutes later.

That wasn't a game – it was a slaughter. His sensible opponent played the opening with profound understanding, thought out his moves with genuine care, and scored a beautiful victory.

Playing the Opening Blindly

The inexperienced player mishandles the opening because he doesn't know what he's doing. He's prone to make one pawn move after another. Why? Because pawn moves are the "simplest." He doesn't realize he's holding up his development, robbing his pieces of their best squares, seriously weakening his position, exposing his king to dangerous attacks.

Take this contrived example of blind opening play (I'll admit it's exaggeratedly ghastly):

Irregular Opening

1.e4 e5

So far, so good. Both players have advanced a center pawn and have created a line of development for the king bishop.

2.d3?

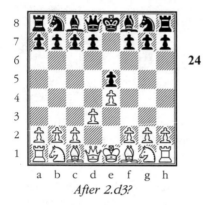

24

After 2.d3?

But this is all wrong! Without being forced to do so, without even being provoked, White voluntarily closes his light-square bishop's line of development.

Never deprive yourself of freedom of action unless you're forced to do so.

But White's 2.d3? was a serious blunder for another reason: timing. He should have played 2.♘f3. *That* move has several points in its favor.

To begin with, it develops a piece. Developed pieces are *active*; they are ready to play an effective role. Pieces left on the first rank are like reserve troops stranded hundreds of miles from the scene of battle.

Note this too: 2.♘f3 is not only a developing move, it's a *forceful* developing move. It attacks Black's e-pawn. Economy of means is the very soul of chess; and what could be more economical than developing with a threat to the enemy?

But 2.♘f3 has still another virtue: it is a *prelude to castling.* Your king is most exposed to attack in the center – that Times Square of the chessboard. Your

king is least exposed to attack when castled – tucked away at the side of the board, where it's not so easy to hack away at his defenses.

Consequently your wisest (most economical) course in the opening is to combine development with early castling. Here's your standard procedure:

(1) Play 1.e4
(2) Play ♘f3
(3) Play out your king bishop.

Now you're ready to castle. *Do it!*

To be sure, this is not a hard and fast rule. You may not succeed in doing these four things in the first four moves. But keep this immediate, concrete, vital goal before you. Achieve it no later than, say, the first ten moves at most. Don't delay; don't forget; don't get sidetracked.

Follow this goal as a matter of course and you'll have splendid prospects for the middlegame. Neglect this goal and you're halfway along the road to losing.

2...♘f6

Excellent: Black develops his king knight to its most effective square. At the same time he makes one of the moves that prepares for castling.

Here is a telltale sign that White has gone wrong: *although White had the first move, Black is ahead in development!*

3.b3?

Another "simple" pawn move. Again White neglects to develop a piece; again he neglects to prepare for castling.

3...d5!

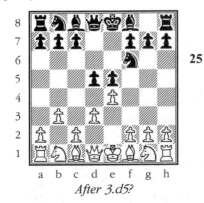

After 3.d5?

By advancing his d-pawn two squares, Black has taken the initiative in the center. At the same time he has opened a diagonal for developing his light-square bishop. This indicates foresight and planning on Black's part.

(Observe that Black doesn't imitate White's mistake by playing 3...d6? – which would deprive Black of the option of later developing his dark-square bishop aggressively.)

But, you may ask, shouldn't Black have developed his dark-square bishop and prepared for immediate castling? A good question.

Early castling would have been quite good for Black, but in this case not absolutely necessary. For White has already limited himself to a *passive* policy and deprived himself of attacking possibilities. Therefore, Black has no immediate need for castling. He can use the time White has offered him on a silver platter in order to seize the initiative in the center.

To get back to the game (Diagram 25). How is White to proceed? If he plays 4.e×d5 there might follow 4...♛×d5, getting another piece into play; (if now 5.♘c3 ♝b4!).

This last bishop move is very fine – a developing move which defends Black's queen by *pinning* White's queen knight. Also, due to the weakening effect of White's second and third pawn moves, Black actually threatens ...♝×c3+, winning a whole rook. (This is a good example of how excessive pawn moves in the opening can weaken your position.)

So, in the position of Diagram 25, White defends. How? Of course, with another "simple" pawn move!

4.f3?

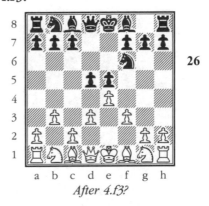

After 4.f3?

White continues to neglect his development. Think of it – *four* moves and not a single piece developed!

Worse yet, White's last move deprives his king knight of his best square: f3. Now the knight must be developed to the side of the board (h3), where a knight has little scope; or to e2, which has two drawbacks:

(1) At e2 the knight is on the second rank and hits out only as far as White's fourth rank. (on f3 the knight is on the third rank and its power extends as far as the fifth rank.) Consequently, ♘e2 is less aggressive than ♘f3.

(2) At e2 the knight blocks the development of White's light-square bishop. Before the bishop can move, it will be necessary for White's knight to make another move, causing further loss of time. Thus ♘e2 is less aggressive – and less economical – than ♘f3.

4...♗c5!

A splendid developing move. Black has increased his lead in development, for he has two pieces out, while White has none.

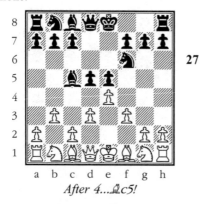

After 4...♗c5!

After his last move Black is ready to castle. But that's not all. By posting his bishop at c5 he monopolizes the diagonal which White has weakened with 4.f3?.

When White succeeds – if he ever does – in laboriously developing his king

knight and light-square bishop, he'll still be unable to castle, because the commanding position of Black's bishop at c5 makes it impossible to station the white king at g1.

Even at this early stage it's not too farfetched to say that White has a lost game. He can never catch up in development; his pieces have no prospect of active, efficient, coordinated operations; his king has no prospect of ultimate safety.

Black, on the other hand, has developed rapidly and freely; he's ready to castle at once; scores of possible plans, all of them good, are at his disposal. He doesn't have to figure out any specific plan. What matters is that he has the potentialities of further purposeful, aggressive play.

If Black continues in the same alert, astute style, the attacks, the threats, the possibilities of winning material will come of themselves. Sooner or later his clear-cut advantages will combine in some profitable aggression that will sweep White from the board. The fate of the game is already foreshadowed.

If you find this statement extreme, consider this perfectly plausible continuation:

5.♗b2 ♘c6

White's developing move attacked the e-pawn; Black's developing reply guarded the pawn.

6.♘e2

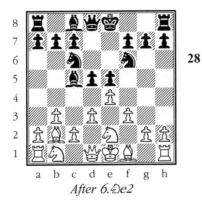

After 6.♘e2

28

White seems to be making headway with his development; actually he is already faced with disaster.

6...d×e4!

A sly move. Whichever way White recaptures he is lost.

7.f×e4

The alternative 7.d×e4 is even worse. (Why?)

7...♘×e4!

With brutal threats of ...♗f2# or ...♘f2, forking queen and rook.

8.d×e4 ♗f2+! 9.♔×f2 ♕×d1 Resigns

White has suffered a crushing material loss. Blame it on the commanding position of Black's bishop at c5 and the feckless pawn moves that ultimately gave Black his chance for a devastating attack.

Playing the Opening by Rote

This may be a bit more sophisticated than playing the opening blindly, but

the results are frequently just as disastrous. The man who plays the opening blindly does so because he doesn't know any better. The man who plays the opening by rote does so despite the fact that he does – or should – know better.

You can't play *any part of the game* well by blindly picking someone else's brains or by unthinkingly making moves dictated solely by custom. It takes only one thoughtless move to ruin even the most perfect position. Danger may lurk in the most harmless-looking situation. For example:

Seppelt – Laeganki
French Defense
Berlin, 1920

1.e4 e6 2.d4 d5 3.♘d2

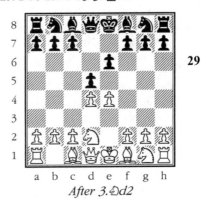

29

After 3.♘d2

White's last move looks suspicious on the face of it, as his queen knight now blocks the development of his dark-square bishop. (He has avoided the more natural-looking 3.♘c3 as he dislikes the pinning reply 3...♗b4.)

When a master plays 3.♘d2, he is well aware of the danger of impeding his development; he sees to it that his queen knight does not linger unduly at d2. A less experienced player, who is merely aping the fashionable 3.♘d2, may easily go wrong.

3...c5 4.e×d5 e×d5 5.d×c5 ♗×c5

What has happened? White exchanged pawns in order to leave Black with an isolated d-pawn. Such a pawn, *which can no longer be guarded by pawns*, must be protected by pieces. In the endgame this weakness can be particularly vexing. But, as Tarrasch loved to point out, "Before the endgame the gods have placed the middlegame." (And, for the benefit of our readers, he should have added, "And before the middlegame they have placed the opening.")

So White is playing positional chess ("just like a master"). Meanwhile he overlooks the fact that he has given Black a fine, free position.

Right now the indicated course is 6.♗b5+ (getting ready to castle); or else 6.♘b3 (driving off Black's advanced bishop, opening the diagonal for his dark-square bishop, and preparing to post the knight at the strong point d4.)

Instead, White blunders horribly:

6.♘e2??

As we've seen, this move is one we must always distrust. The knight is less aggressive here than at f3 and it blocks the development of White's light-square bishop.

6...♕b6! Resigns

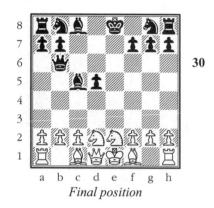

Final position

Black threatens 7...♗×f2#. Both 7.f3 and 7.♘b3 still allow mate.* So White has nothing better than 7.♘d4, staving off the mate by losing a piece.

Preoccupied with highfalutin strategical ideas, White has left his king wide open to sudden and disastrous attack.

Unforeseen Crisis

The player who makes his moves by rote is putting implicit faith in the book. What book? Well, whatever book happens to be in fashion at the time. The books change, the recommended moves give way to other moves recommended just as strongly. Yet the attitude of the man who plays by rote – the man who relies on authority – remains the same. He continues to accept the current book moves without trying to fathom the reasons behind them.

The right way to play the opening is to use your own judgment, even if it involves making mistakes. It takes maturity to do this and to rely on it. But it's the only way to improve.

When you succeed you get the pleasure of winning by your own efforts, and you gain confidence. Even when you lose you learn what to avoid.

What's more, by using your own judgment, you're less likely to be confronted with unforeseen crises – like this one:

Queen's Gambit Declined

1.d4 d5 2.c4 e6 3.♘c3 ♘f6 4.♗g5

The most popular moves here are 4...♘bd7 or 4...♗e7. Both have been tested over the years, and to most of us it's a matter of indifference which one we play first. Very often, indeed, they transpose into the same position.

You may conclude, therefore, that either move can be played "without a thought." But that's not so! If Black plays 4...♗e7 the opening takes a sedate, uneventful course. But if he plays 4...♘bd7 – objectively at least as good – he *may* suddenly find himself in trouble.

4...♘bd7

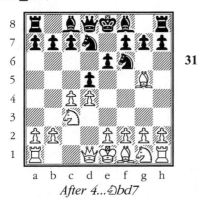

After 4...♘bd7

Black has played a perfectly routine move and feels quite satisfied with his position.

Suddenly he sees to his horror that White can win a pawn by 5.c×d5 e×d5 6.♘×d5. (Black's king knight is pinned!)

How did Black come to overlook this rather obvious point? Because he relied on his recollections of other people's moves, recorded in books. Consequently he has rattled off the opening moves glibly – without thought, without intention, without plan, and, worst of all, without reason.

Now, at last, Black applies himself desperately to see what can be done against the threatened pawn loss. And this is what he finds:

5.c×d5 e×d5 6.♘×d5??

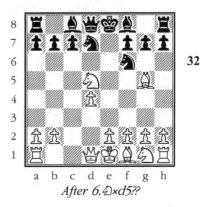

After 6.♘×d5??

6...♘×d5!!

A beautiful example of the magnificent resources often hidden in barren-looking positions. But you must look for them!

7.♗×d8 ♗b4+ 8.♕d2 ♗×d2+ 9.♔×d2 ♔×d8

And Black has won a piece.

Black was lucky in this case. It's not often that the "routineeer," as Tarrasch calls him, is fortunate enough to escape the consequences of his routine play. The next example shows how a player is typically punished for handling the opening thoughtlessly.

Crime and Punishment

This example involves one of the most popular – and one of the least understood – variations in the whole repertoire of opening play. This is the Morphy Defense to the Ruy Lopez, beginning with the moves 1.e4 e5 2.♘f3 ♘c6 3.♗b5 a6.

Is Black's last move good or bad? Apparently very few players have asked themselves this question. I know players who've been using this defense for 30 years without learning to this day the purpose behind 3...a6. So, let's see if we can discover that purpose:

Ruy Lopez Morphy Defense

1.e4 e5 2.♘f3 ♘c6 3.♗b5

33

After 3.♗b5

White threatens – or seems to threaten – to win a pawn by ♗×c6 and ♘×e5.

Black's problem is to make a move that will keep his e-pawn guarded and that also will contribute to a general plan of development.

Most modern masters are agreed that 3...a6 (The Morphy Defense) is the answer to Black's problems. He need not fear 4.♗×c6 in reply, for after 4...d×c6 5.♘×e5 he regains the lost material in satisfactory fashion by 5...♕d4 or 5...♕g5 (double attack in either case).

So Black drives off White's bishop and at the same time avoids material loss. After the further moves 4.♗a4 ♘f6 5.0-0 the game may follow either one of these two important trunk lines:
(a) 5...♗e7 6.♖e1 b5 7.♗b3 d6 8.c3 0-0 9.h3 ♘a5 10.♗c2 c5 11.d4 ♕c7!. By means of his space-gaining ninth and tenth moves Black has given his queen a good post and generally freed his game.
(b) 5...♘×e4 6.d4 b5 7.♗b3 d5 8.d×e5 ♗e6 Here too Black has established good posts for his pieces.

In both variations Black's bid for freedom depends on his driving back White's bishop. There you have Black's basic strategy.

To return to Diagram 33: Black decides on a different type of development, beginning with:

3...♘f6

So Black has veered away from the Morphy Defense (3...a6), at least for the time being. The move he's chosen certainly looks promising: he develops a piece and counterattacks on White's e-pawn. And, as we've seen, he needn't worry about the fate of his e-pawn at this point.

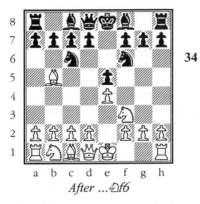

After ...♘f6

4.0-0

White is not concerned about his e-pawn, for after 4...♘xe4 he will undermine the position of the advanced knight with 5.d4 (so that if 5...exd4? 6.♖e1, and Black is in serious trouble because of the pin on the e-file.)

However, this is by no means the last word on the consequences of 4...♘xe4. Black can play this move safely – if he prudently answers 5.d4 with 5...♗e7, developing another piece, removing all danger on the e-file, and getting ready to castle.

Instead, Black, who hasn't examined this possibility because he's playing by rote, decides on 4...a6 for his next move. After all, he says to himself, I get the same position from 1.e4 e5 2.♘f3 ♘c6 3.♗b5 ♘f6 4.0-0 a6 5.♗a4 ♗e7 as from the standard book line 1.e4 e5 2.♘f3 ♘c6 3.♗b5 a6 4.♗a4 ♘f6 5.0-0 ♗e7.

On the face of it, there seems to be nothing wrong with Black's play. Apparently there is no harm in his slight change in the order of his moves (3...♘f6 instead of the standard 3...a6 and then 4...a6 instead of the standard

4...♘f6). But – as you'll soon see – there is a very definite reason for the sequence of the standard book moves.

4...a6?

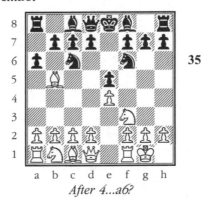

After 4...a6?

Black is so eager to drive off the bishop that he overlooks the possible loss of his e-pawn.

What he fails to take into account is that, *given the changed order of his third and fourth moves, White's king rook is poised for action in the center.* Result: White wins a pawn – the e-pawn that has been neglected.

5.♗xc6!

Unlike his opponent, White cleverly accommodates himself to the changed circumstances.

5...dxc6 6.♘xe5

And White has won a pawn for keeps.

Thus, if 6...♕d4? White simply replies 7.♘f3, and if 7...♕xe4??? 8.♖e1 wins the queen.

Or if 6...♘xe4?? 7.♖e1 and White wins material: a retreat of the menaced knight allows a decisive discovered check on the e-file. Nor will it do to protect the knight (7...♘f5 8.d3 etc.).

The moral this example drives home is clear. To play the opening with a general plan in mind is good, but you must not rush through the individual moves that make up that planned course of play. Think about each move; study the possibilities it creates for your opponent; satisfy yourself that it doesn't expose you to loss of material.

What you've seen in this chapter, then, is that playing the opening blindly only stirs up future misery for you. Thoughtless pawn moves hinder your development, leave your king exposed to attack, or else allow your opponent to get a magnificent lead in development.

So, avoid playing the opening blindly. Bring out your pieces rapidly and effectively. Castle early. Be wary of excessive pawn moves.

And remember, too, that playing the opening by rote may lead to the same sad consequences. Make sure that general rules hold good in specific positions. In other words: don't make opening moves without seeing their underlying purpose. Don't be content with taking someone else's word for the merits of a move. Don't play a move without having a reason for it.

And, above all, remember that *good plans and bad timing* are just as bad as having no plan at all.

Chapter 3

You Don't Know the One Basic Principle of Chess Play: Control the Center

To understand the importance of the center and to know how to control it are the marks of a good player. For such control is the key to a winning attack.

And that's not all. Control of the center enables you to obtain superior mobility, to develop your pieces powerfully, to restrict the development of your opponent's pieces.

So you see the center is vitally important. Yet it's unfortunately true that most chess books have either ignored it or dismissed it with a platitude or two.

The result? What's good enough for the book is good enough for you, so you do the same thing. Don't tell me different. I wouldn't believe you. And that's one important reason why you lose at chess.

Here's what you need to know:
(1) What is the center?
(2) How do you control the center?
(3) Why is it important to control the center?

What is the center?

The center is an area of central squares. It is made up of the basic center (the squares marked with an X in Diagram 36) and the subsidiary center (the squares marked with a + in Diagram 36).

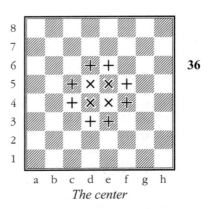

36

The center

The basic center squares are e4, e5, d4, d5.

The basic center pawns are the e-pawn and the d-pawn.

The subsidiary center squares are f4, f5, c4, c5, e3, d3, e6, d6.

The subsidiary center pawns are the f-pawn and the c-pawn.

How do you control the center?

There are basically three ways to control the center:
(1) By occupying the center with pawns.
(2) By occupying the center with pieces.
(3) By striking at and/or through the center with pieces.

Often you can use these methods simultaneously.

Why is it important to control the center?

In this sense we user "center" to mean the basic center. Just why do we place such enormous value on controlling the center?

Simply because it's here that your pieces have their greatest scope. Place a queen on any one of the four center squares and you'll see she has more potential squares to go to than from any other position on the board. The same applies to other pieces as well.

Let's look at some examples:

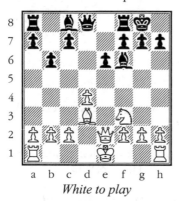

White to play

White unleashes the enormous power of the queen by playing **1.♕e4!**. This attacks to the right (threatening 2.♕×h7#) and also to the left (threatening 2.♕×a8).

Black must guard against the mate and therefore loses his queen rook by force.

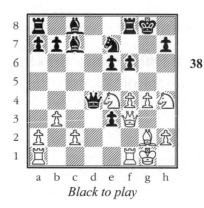

38

Black to play

In Diagram 38 we again observe the power of the centralized queen:

Black plays **1...e2+**, attacking the king rook. White must lose a rook! If he tries to save the menaced king rook by **2.♖f2**, then comes **2...♕×a1+** (attacking in another direction), and Black wins.

The powerful placement of a white rook in Diagram 39 illustrates another occupation of the center by pieces. The real theme, however, is the power of the pieces striking *through* the center.

Reinfeld – Enzinger
Marshall Chess Club Championship
1926

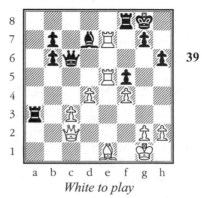

39

White to play

You Don't Know the One Basic Principle of Chess Play: Control the Center

At first glance you might think that Black, with his pressure against the c-pawn, has the initiative.

Actually this isn't so. White's rooks have a strangle hold on the vital open center file. The rook at e7 has a powerful grip on the seventh rank.

However, White's queen and bishop are not very active. How can they add to the pressure? The answer calls for aggressive action in the center by White. Therefore:

1.♕b2!!

The underlying idea of this move is to strike with the queen through the center at the g7-square! This seems fantastic, but it is merely an example of how powerfully a piece can work if it *strikes through the center*.

If I had fully understood the value of the center at the time this game was played, I might have found this rather subtle move more quickly. But I was only 16 at the time and somewhat hazy about the importance of the center.

1...♖aa8 2.d5!

White clears away one of the obstacles blocking the diagonal to g7. And he does it with a gain of time by attacking Black's queen!

2...♕d6 3.c4!

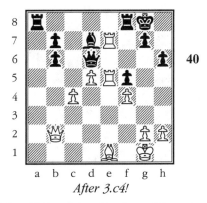

After 3.c4!

Now White shows his claws. His main threat is 4.♖×g7+! ♚×g7 5.♖e7+ ♚g6 6.♖g7+ ♚h5 7.♕e2#.

There is also an additional menace: 4.♖5e6 winning Black's queen because of the unmasked mate threat along the diagonal.

These threats give us a striking idea of the power that pieces develop when they operate through the center.

Now back to Diagram 40. What is Black to do? He sees that 3...♖f7 is worthless, for then comes 4.♗b4 ♕c7 5.♖×f7 ♚×f7 6.♖e7+ and it's all over.

And if 4...♕f6 5.♖×f7 ♚×f7 6.♖e7+; or 5...♕×f7 6.♖e7 and wins.

3...♖f6

Last try; he hopes to block the disastrous diagonal.

4.♗b4

In preparation for what is to follow, White prevents the black queen from guarding the black king rook.

4...♕c7 5.♖×f5!

43

After 5.♖xf5!

42

Black to play

White has forced his opponent into a neat double pin: if 5...♖xf5 6.♕xg7♯; or if 5...♗xf5 6.♖xc7.

5...♖a2

Even 5...♖af8 would not have prevented White's next move.

6.♖xg7+! Resigns

The culmination of White's attack through the center.

From these examples we can see that a player who has control of the center has an enormous advantage. On the other hand, a player with a feeble grip on the center will in all likelihood find his pieces miserably huddled together, denied access to their most favorable squares.

The last thought suggest that center pawns can perform a magnificent restraining job. We've already seen in the previous chapter that center pawns open up lines of development by their advance. Let's now observe how a strong pawn center can deprive our opponent's forces of mobility:

The outlook for Black here is dismal, thanks to White's all-powerful center. Thus, Black cannot gain a foothold in the center with ...e5 or ...c5, both of these moves being prevented by White's d-pawn in cooperation with White's knight.*

White's knight has access to the powerful central square e5. Black's knight, on the other hand, cannot execute the same maneuver; nor is ...♘d5 possible, as White's e-pawn stands guard over the d5-square.

To sum up: White's control of the center gives him an obviously superior game. He can gradually strengthen his position and face the future with confidence. Black's weak grip on the center gives him an uncomfortably passive game, condemned to a policy of "wait-and-see."

The Powerful Pawn Center

The following game shows how a powerful pawn center helps your own development, hampers your opponent's development, and leads to constriction of his game so that successful defense becomes impossible for him.

Roudolph – Amateur
King's Gambit
New York 1912

1.e4 e5 2.f4

A struggle for control of the center. White hopes to remove the black e-pawn's command of the center. If White is successful, he will be able to play d2-d4 with a formidable pawn center.

2...e×f4 3.♗c4

With this developing move White intensifies his control of the important d5-square and also strikes through the center at f7, which is often a vulnerable point in Black's game.

3...♗c5?

A developing move – but not a good one. For White's biff-bang reply shows that he means to remain master of the center.

4.d4!

43

After 4.d4!

White's last move illustrates the classic role of the powerful pawn center in depriving hostile pieces access to the center.

4...♕h4+

Black sets a little trap that has short-term value and is otherwise worthless in the long run. He hopes for 5.g3? when 5...f×g3 gives him a winning game because of the murderous threat ...g2+.

However, White sees through this flimsy plan and soon furthers his own development by attacking Black's queen with gain of time.

5.♔f1

White's loss of castling does no harm because Black is in no position to take advantage of it.

5...♗b6 6.♘f3 ♕d8 7.♗×f4

Now White has superb development and his pieces bear down powerfully on the center. Black would like to play 7...♘f6, but in that case the reply 8.e5 drives the knight away. (Another example of the way a powerful pawn center restricts the opponent's possibilities of development.)

7...♘e7

Being debarred from playing the best developing move (...♘f6), Black is compelled to adopt a more passive line.

But now White embarks on a powerful attack:

8.♘g5

After 8.♘g5

44

After 10...♔h8

45

The time has come for Black to pay for his past sins. If he tries to hit back in the center to break the attack on his f-pawn there follows: 8...d5 9.e×d5 ♘×d5 10.♘×f7! ♔×f7 11.♕h5+. Now Black loses quickly whether he plays 11...♔e6 12.♕e5+ etc. or 11...g6 12.♗×d5+ etc.

So Black tries another way, but White's attack is too much for him.

8...0-0 9.♕h5

This crushing attacking move is made possible by Black's failure to play ...♘f6 – and this in turn may be credited to White's powerful pawn center. (See note to White's seventh move.)

9...h6 10.♗×f7+ ♔h8

Allowing a brilliant finish, but after 10...♖×f7 11.♕×f7+ he is hopelessly behind in material.

11.♕×h6+! g×h6 12.♗e5 #

Significantly, White checkmates with a centralized bishop! This suggests our next theme.

The Powerfully Centralized Piece

We've already seen the strength of a powerfully centralized piece in Diagrams 37 and 38. In the following example White gets a very powerful game because of his formidably centralized knight on e5.

Pillsbury – Marco
Queen's Gambit Declined
Paris 1900

1.d4 d5 2.c4 e6 3.♘c3 ♘f6 4.♗g5 ♗e7 5.e3 0-0 6.♘f3 b6 7.♗d3 ♗b7 8.c×d5 e×d5

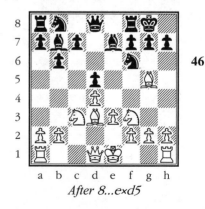

46

After 8...e×d5

Both players have developed their forces quickly, but White's game is somewhat freer. This is due mainly to the fact that his bishop at d3 strikes through the center at Black's kingside, whereas the black bishop at b7 is blocked by the d5-pawn.

9.♘e5!

This is the famous move with which the great Pillsbury won some beautiful games in striking style. The impact of these victories was such that the defense adopted here by Black eventually went out of style.

The chief technical factor in Pillsbury's wins was the *powerfully centralized position* of the knight at e5.

Here the knight is ideally placed, and his power radiates out toward the kingside and the queenside as well. White proceeds with f2-f4 and ♕f3, followed by ♕h3, working up a formidable attack.

With best play Black can probably defend himself adequately. But he must look sharp and waste no opportunities. In practice, as Pillsbury proved, this line favors the attacker – mostly because of his strongly centralized knight at e5.

Striking though the Center

Some of the most beautiful combinations ever made are found, on careful examination, to be due to an attack through the center. (As I keep stressing, if *you* control the center, this attack is blunted.) We've already seen such a long-distance attack in Diagram 39, but the two following Anderssen gems are prettier:

Anderssen – Amateur
Evans Gambit
Breslau, 1860

1.e4 e5 2.♘f3 ♘c6 3.♗c4 ♗c5 4.b4 ♗×b4 5.c3 ♗c5 6.0-0 d6 7.d4 e×d4 8.c×d4 ♗b6 9.d5

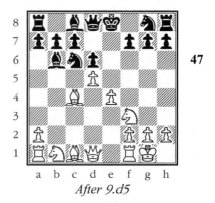

After 9.d5

Anderssen's favorite move. At the cost of closing the light-square bishop's diagonal, he opens the line for the other bishop, which will now strike through the center at the g7-square.

9...♘a5 10.♗b2 ♘f6 11.♗d3 ♗g4 12.♘c3 c6 13.♘e2

White shifts the knight, partly to use it with good effect on the kingside, partly to keep the diagonal open for his dark-square bishop.

13...0-0 14.♕d2

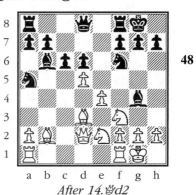

After 14.♕d2

It's dangerously easy for Black to go wrong in this position if he neglects the long-distance effect of the white dark-square bishop.

Another famous Anderssen game, for example, would up like this: 14...♖c8 15.♕g5 ♗xf3 16.gxf3 cxd5 17.♔h1! ♘c4 18.♖g1 ♘e8 and now White reveals the power of the long-range bishop striking through the center: 19.♕xg7+!! ♘xg7 20.♖xg7+ ♔h8 21.♖g8+!! ♔xg8 22.♖g1+ ♕g5 23.♖xg5#!

14...♘d7 15.♕f4 ♗h5 16.♘g3 ♗g6 17.♖ad1 cxd5 18.exd5 ♘c5 19.♘f5 ♘xd3?

Black is all unsuspecting. He soon finds out that the long-range bishop is not to be trifled with.

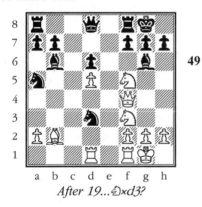

After 19...♘xd3?

20.♕h6!! Resigns

For if 20...gxh6 21.♘xh6# – thanks to the bishop and its ferocious diagonal that cuts right through the center.

You're bothered by unusual openings

You may wonder what this has to do with the subject we're discussing – the importance of the center. It has everything to do with it.

Unusual openings, so called, are unusual only in that they ignore the center. Most frequently they're employed by weaker players who think they'll confuse you by "taking you out of the book." All too frequently they succeed. And so you lose.

Instead of letting yourself be confused, recognize these moves for what they are – bad moves. And while your opponents are fumbling around with their "unusual moves," grab the center yourself and eat roast duck.

Here's a particularly graphic example of this point, because it shows the absurdity of trying to fool a first-rate opponent with "unusual" opening moves. (Morphy, who plays White here, is playing eight blindfold games simultaneously.)

Morphy – Carr
Irregular Defense
Birmingham, 1858

1.e4 h6? 2.d4 a5?

Black's idiotic, "unusual" moves have allowed White to establish a pawn monopoly in the center. Even at this early stage White can look forward confidently to the middlegame, secure in the knowledge that the black pieces will never find good squares.

3.♗d3 b6 4.♘e2 e6 5.0-0 ♗a6 6.c4!

Of course, when you have much more terrain than your opponent, you don't allow him to exchange his badly-posted pieces for your well-posted pieces.

6...♘f6 7.e5!

Here is the perfect example of how pawn monopoly of the center allows you to drive off hostile pieces from that vital area.

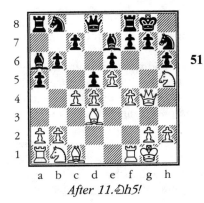

After 11.♘h5!

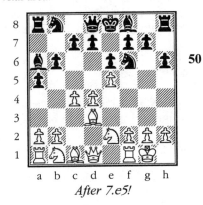

After 7.e5!

7...♘h7

Both black "developed" pieces are posted miserably. Blame it on his neglect of the center.

8.f4 ♗e7 9.♘g3 d5 10.♕g4!

White's superior development, resulting from control of the center, allows him to go over to direct attack. Now 10...g6 would be too weakening. So Black castles – but not into safety.

10...0-0 11.♘h5!

White threatens mate, and 11...g6 won't do because of 12.♗xg6 etc.

11...g5 12.fxg5

Now Black can't recapture with a piece because of 13.h4 winning a piece.

12...hxg5 13.♗xh7+ ♚h8

Or "resigns." If 13...♚xh7 14.♘f6+ ♗xf6 15.♖xf6 and White has a mating attack.

14.♘f6 dxc4 15.♗c2

Now 15.♗e4 forces an immediate win. But Morphy's way is good enough.

15...♕xd4+

Losing a second piece in order to ward off White's threat of mate in two moves. The rest doesn't matter (16.♕xd4 ♗c5 17.♕xc5 etc.). Black is hopelessly behind in material.

This game follows a pattern which appears often in games between unevenly matched players. The sequence is:
    (1) Control the center
    (2) Better development
    (3) Decisive attack

By gaining control of the center, White obtains a magnificent development for his pieces, while Black's forces are correspondingly constricted. The resulting lead in development gives White a sharp initiative which in turn leads to a crushing attack.

But even in games between evenly matched players, an unusual opening will lead to disaster because it neglects the center. Here is an example:

Dunst – Reinfeld
Nimzovich Attack (in effect)
Marshall Chess Club Championship
1929

1.e3

A mysterious move – the kind that often fills the opponent with panic because it leads to the unknown and uncharted.

However, Black is not impressed. He reasons that 1.e3 commands less of the center than 1.e4 and must therefore be a weaker move. Furthermore, he sees a certain trend in 1.e3 which he's determined to combat – an indication that White means to maneuver and hedge, revealing his plans very tardily.

Instead of being scared by this policy of mystification, Black falls in with it by making an apparently even more noncommittal reply.

Don't think, however, that Black is ignoring the center. Remember we saw on page 41 that there are three ways to control the center:
    (1) By occupying the center with pawns
    (2) By occupying the center with pieces

    (3) By striking at and/or through the center with pieces.

White, as you've seen, has abdicated his role of being the first to have a try at controlling the center. Thus he leaves the choice to Black.

Black decides on the third method: *he will use his pieces to control the center.* As this game progresses, control with the pieces is highly effective when the other player has renounced any attempt at pawn control.

1...♘f6

Black leaves his opponent in the dark as to his plans for the center pawns.

2.♘f3 g6

More of the same. Black will fianchetto his dark-square bishop and castle, still leaving the center pawns untouched. (And why not? Due to his tacitly announced holding-back policy in the center, White is in no position to undertake action in the center.)

3.b3 ♗g7 4.♗b2 0-0

Now two fianchettoed bishops dispute control of the long diagonal. In effect, there is a long-range duel of the two bishops striking at each other through the center. All this may impress you as too portentous and slow moving. But, since Black is in no danger, why shouldn't he be calm and unhurried in planning his development?

5.♗e2 b6 6.0-0 c5 7.♘e5 ♗b7 8.♗f3

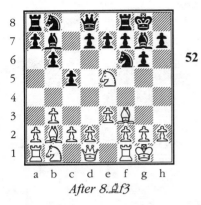

After 8.♗f3

52

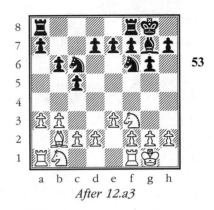

After 12.a3

53

Black has fianchettoed his remaining bishop to strike at the center. White neutralizes this pressure and at the same time offers an exchange of bishops. Some players would automatically reject the exchange by playing ...d5. But Black reasons otherwise in this game: he proposes to let White have his way in all objectives that have no real value. For White is bound to reach a dead end because he has ignored the problem of controlling the center.

8...♕c7 9.♗×b7 ♕×b7 10.♕f3

Here the previous note applies. Black is perfectly content to let White carry out his intentions. Such a sequence of uninspired ideas can only leave White with a distressing lack of initiative.

10...♕×f3 11.♘×f3 ♘c6

Development with gain of time, as ...♘b4 promises to be annoying.

12.a3

Now we can sense, perhaps without being able to put it into words, that White's game is uncomfortable.

12...♖fe8

This move points to a future ...e7-e5-e4. What is White to do about it?

If he tries 13.♘e5, then 13...♘g4! gives Black a splendid game.

Or if 13.d4 ♘e4! and the pin on White's d-pawn gives Black a decided initiative.

13.d3 d5

Black decides on a broad pawn advance in the center, as White cannot very well proceed with 14.♘e5 or 14.d4.

14.♘bd2 e5!

Poetic justice! White has consistently ignored the center, and now Black takes the initiative there. The tranquil methods pursued by Black are very instructive, for they emphasize how much White loses by neglecting the center.

After 14...e5!

54

Now White is faced with such grim possibilities as ...e4, putting his king knight out of action, or ...d4, burying his bishop.

15.e4

The irony of it all! At last, after many tortuous moves, White plays the advance he might have had, without any concessions to Black, on the very first move!

And – sadder yet – at this point the play with the e-pawn has a flaw: it allows the inroad of Black's queen knight.

15...♘d4!

A cruel dilemma for White. If he leaves this knight on the board, it is actively and annoyingly centralized. In addition, it attacks the c-pawn, and ♖(either)c1? will not do because of ...♘e2+.

55

After 15...♘d4!

White has been reduced to such a pass by his neglect of the easy solutions. He gets rid of the knight – but at a heavy price, as you will see.

16.♘×d4 c×d4!

Now a new difficulty appears for White: a backward c-pawn which can be attacked by Black's rooks on the c-file. So White hastens to rid himself of this embarrassing weakness.

17.c3 d×c3 18.♗×c3 ♖ac8!

Black presses his advantage relentlessly. If now 19.♗b2 ♖c2 20.♗c1 and White is helpless.

19.♖ac1

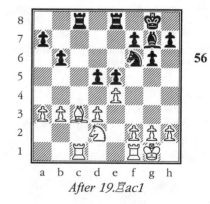

After 19.♖ac1

56

Having ignored the center, White finds himself condemned to defeat.

19...♗h6!

Decisive! Black threatens to win a piece by 21...d4 22.♗b4 a5. It's White's misfortune that his bishop is rooted to its present square.

20.f4?!

Desperation. After 20.♖fd1 Black has many ways to establish a decisive positional advantage, for example 20...d4 21.♗b2 ♖xc1 22.♗xc1 ♖c8 (intending ...♖c2 or ...♖c3).

Or 20...dxe4 21.dxe4 ♖ed8 and White can't hold out.

**20...♗xf4 21.g3 ♗e3+! 22.♔g2 d4!
Resigns**

For if 23.♖xf6, 23...dxc3 wins more material.

And if 23.♗b2, 23...♗xd2 24.♖xc8 ♖xc8 25.♖xf6 ♖c2 26.♗a1 ♗c3+ wins the unlucky bishop.

So I say it again – control the center; occupy the center; strike *through* the center. That's your battleground. Grab it!

When General Forrest was asked his advice on military tactics, he replied: "Git thar fustest with the mostest." This maxim makes equally good chess tactics. Remember, the center is your battleground. So get there fastest with the most, and you'll soon cease to ask yourself: Why do I lose at chess?

Chapter 4

You Lose Because You Can't See One Move Ahead

This is a harsh indictment.

You'll probably resent it. Who wouldn't?

Okay, let's try a simple test.

Gilbert – Murray
Minnesota Championship 1946

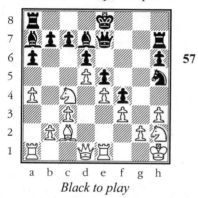

57

Black to play

Black is a pawn down. Still, the position is blocked and it won't be easy for White to make use of his extra pawn.

Moreover, Black has strong bishops and an open g-file. It would appear then that he has attacking chances.

How should Black proceed?

Should he castle and then swing his queen rook over to the g-file?

Should he find open lines for his bishops?

Should he seek attacking positions for his queen?

The answer to all these questions is simple. Black should do none of these things. Instead, in the position of Diagram 57 he should go right ahead and play 1...♘g3#!

I've frequently shown this innocent-looking position to students, and I've been repeatedly astonished to see how often they overlook the one-move checkmate. Did you?

Why do you miss so obvious a move? Because your entire attention is focused on a plan – a whole series of moves.

Planning is fine. I'm all for it. But each move is important in itself. It may win the game for you – or it could ruin your position.

Chess masters are aware of this. You think of a master as one who can see far, far ahead. I prefer to think of a master as one who in any given position will almost invariably find the strongest move.

What impresses us is that he will find the strongest move even when it is quite hidden in a harmless-looking position. Take this innocent setting:

Rossolimo – Wood
Southsea, 1949

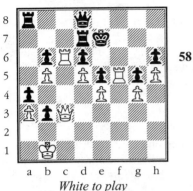

White to play

Spielmann – Leonhardt
San Sabastian, 1912

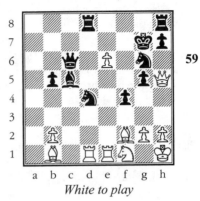

White to play

White is a pawn down, but Black's pieces are poorly posted and his king is in some danger. White has all the play, yet nothing decisive seems available. The game has already gone on for 86 moves – the kind of play that involves a lot of backing and filling and waiting. Endless waiting. In such games, as you know, one's attention is easily lulled.

But Rosolimo sees his chance:

1.♕xe5+!!! dxe5 2.♖e6#!

And here is another example that impressed me. I was playing over a game of Spielmann's in which that great master of the attack reached the following position:

What is White's next move?

Without looking at the score, and in fact without any thought at all, I reached out and played:

1.e7!

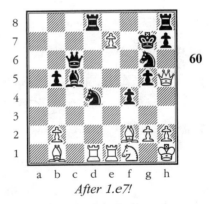

After 1.e7!

Then, looking at the score, I saw that this was indeed the move Spielman had played.

Why did I play that move? Frankly, because it looked strong. But my instinct was sound, for the move wins by force.

The reason I advanced the pawn intuitively was that it attacks Black's queen rook, which is tied to the d-file to guard Black's knight at d4. Thus, if 1...♖de8 White replies 2.♗xd4+, winning a piece.

But, you will say, the pawn at e7 can be captured by Black's bishop or knight. Not so fast – remember, Black's bishop is also tied to the defense of the knight at d4!

This means that 1...♗xe7 will not do at all, as the reply 2.♗xd4+ or 2.♖xd4 wins the knight.

But 1...♘xe7 will not do either, for then 2.♗xd4+ ♖xd4 3.♖xd4 ♗xd4 4.♖xe7+ forces mate next move.

So we see that 1.e7! is possible because of the badly "hanging" position of Black's advanced knight.

Black realized all this, and played:

1...♖d6

If 1...♖d5 2.♗xg6 and wins, for if 2...♕xg6 3.♕xg6+ and 4.e8♕(+).

2.♗xg6 hxg6 3.♕xh8+! Resigns

For White will queen and come out a rook ahead.

The moral is that each move is a challenge. You must be ever alert for the strongest move – one that wins material, one that puts pressure on your opponent. Conversely, the strongest move may be one that attends to the safety of your own king.

This is an art that can't be learned in a day. It is a skill that requires patience and perseverance. But it is a worthwhile skill. If you think back, you will recall many promising games that you spoiled by one unwary move, or by blindly pursuing a long-range "plan."

You're obsessed by the "obvious" move

To be on guard against blunders is not enough. You must also distrust moves that are obvious, as well as decisions that are obvious.

This is particularly urgent when you embark on a variation (sequence of moves). The moves may all be obvious; yet one of them may contain a gruesome flaw.

That's why a strong player is less interested in the length of a variation than he is in the soundness of each individual move in it. He knows that a variation, like a chain, is no stronger than its weakest link. He knows that a player working out a combination – a series of moves – must proceed delicately like a man mounting a rickety staircase, pausing carefully at each step to make sure the next board will bear his weight.

When you fail to observe these precautions, you go astray. With your gaze fixed on far-off horizons, you overlook what is literally under your very nose. So, don't try to be fancy, especially when you're up against a keen tactician. Keep it simple. Profit by learning from White's mistake in the following position.

Solomon – Bernstein
Montevideo 1954

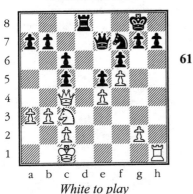

61

White to play

White is two pawns down and he has a weak e-pawn, unprotected by any white pawns. He is condemned to passivity – not an inviting prospect. So, attacking the black pawn at c5, he decides to be cute. As a diversion he tries:

1.♘a4?

Black can defend simply enough by 1...b6, but he has a much better move:

1...b5!!

This move looks nonsensical, as White can (seemingly) save everything with:

2.♕xc5

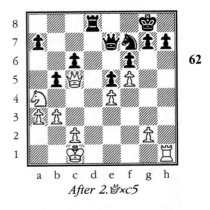

62

After 2.♕xc5

At this point you can picture White looking complacently around at the kibitzers. His two-move variation works – or so it seems – because Black's queen is *en prise*. (If 2...♕xc5 3.♘xc5 and White has won the pawn safely.

2...♖d6!!

Beautiful play, completely knocking out White's obvious variation. White must now lose his knight, for if 3.♘c3 (or 3.♘b2) 3...♖d1+! wins White's queen. There we have the flaw in White's variation made up of obvious moves. So White resigns.

No wonder old Tarrasch used to cry out in strident despair: *"You must see it! You must see it!"* To one student who wanted to know how to avoid mistakes, he said grimly: "Sit on your hands."

Just as you must beware of obvious moves, you must also beware of obvious decisions. If you look ahead one move, you will not prove as gullible as Black did in the following position:

Reshevsky – Mastichiadis
Dubrovnik Team Tournament 1950

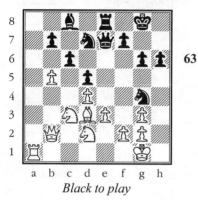

63

Black to play

Black's position looks miserable.

White is about to play b×c6, and after Black replies ...b×c6 he will be left with a backward pawn on an open file. White will gain a lot of space with ♖a7 and then hammer away at the weak pawn with such moves as ♘b3-a5 etc.

So reasons Black, blind to his opportunity. Suddenly he hears Reshevsky offer a draw! Why not? Greatly relieved, Black hastily accepts, without bothering to ask himself why Reshevsky has suddenly become a philanthropist.

Yet if Black had not been so busy studying the dreary, long-term prospects of his weak c-pawn, he might have been less befuddled by Reshevsky's canny offer.

In fact, if Black had been searching for the strongest move, he might have seen:

1...♘×f2!

Now White's position is shattered. His bishop is attacked, and if 2.♔×f2 ♕×e3+ followed by 3...♕×d3+ wins easily for him.

So Black missed his grand opportunity, but at least he was lucky(?) enough to escape with a draw.

In the next example, the play is even more curious. Here one player loses because of his blunder, the other wins because of *his*.

Capablanca – Thomas
Hastings Victory Tournament 1919

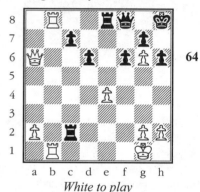

64

White to play

This is the kind of position – like the one in Diagram 63 – that lends itself to instinctive appraisal. The difference between the two positions is that here you have to back up the instinctive appraisal with some hard thinking.

A quick look tells us these things:

White's pieces are aggressive. Black's are passive.

Worse yet for Black, the pawn wedge on g6 leaves Black's king in a mating position on the first rank.

Such a position ought to be child's play for Capablanca, the "chess machine." He can win easily with:

1.♖×e8!

An easy enough move to see, as the reply is forced.

1...♕×e8 2.♕a4!!

This is a bit harder to see, and yet not too hard. Certainly not too hard for Capablanca, perhaps the greatest single-move player in chess history. It involves a double attack, menacing Black's queen and rook, and taking advantage of the black king's mating vulnerability.

The point is that if 2...♕×a4 3.♖b8+ leads to mate. Thus Black must part with his rook, so he might as well resign.

But the "chess machine" did not play this line. Instead (Diagram 64) he continued:

1.♕a8??

The idea is that if 1...♖×b8 (what else?) 2.♖×b8 Black is mated no matter what he does.

Convinced – in fact, overwhelmed – Thomas resigned without looking any further.

And yet he had a won game!

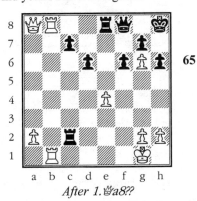

8
7
6 65
5
4
3
2
1

a b c d e f g h

After 1.♕a8??

How? Simply by playing:

1...♖×a2!!

If now 2.♖×e8 ♖×a8 3.♖×f8+ ♔×f8 and Black is in no danger, with a pawn to the good.

Or 2.♕×a2 ♖×b8 with the same result.

But, you may say, this is rather involved; there are several ways to go wrong. Besides, as Thomas probably explained ruefully, "You don't expect Capablanca to blunder." But how can anyone ever find the right move with that type of reasoning?

Even in much simpler situations such reasoning may prove fatal. For example:

Von Popiel – Marco
Monte Carlo 1902

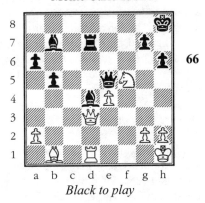

66

a b c d e f g h

Black to play

Black finds himself in what *seems* to be an unfortunate position: his dark-square bishop, attacked three times and defended only twice, is rooted to the spot. It is pinned and therefore cannot move.

Note that tricky word "therefore." Remember what we said about a variation being no stronger than its weakest link? Generally propositions frequently have their exceptions. And exceptions invariably rule out the obvious.

Here is one of the exceptions:

1...♗g1!!

This wins, as Black threatens ...♕×h2‡ and also attacks White's queen. White must lose his queen or suffer equally grievous material loss.

Now surely, you will say, Marco, the greatest annotator of them all, saw this resource and saved the game?

No, not at all. He resigned!

His mind, you see, was too rigidly attuned to long variations, to profound appraisals, to far-reaching plans. The immediate job, the simple task, the most pressing need – in short, *the very next move* – was beyond his all-too-complicated ken.

Beware the Forced Move

The more ingenious a combination is, the more pleasure it gives us. Perhaps there is a sense of power involved in constructing a whole series of forced moves that our opponent is powerless to alter.

But – as you've seen – these forced variations can be dangerous if you don't constantly bear in mind that they can easily topple over. You need a sense of proportion, a constant, watchful awareness that your opponent has something to say about these moves.

The following example from Alekhine's youthful period is fascinating in a psychological sense. A year or two later Alekhine was to be a world-famous master. But at the time this game was played he was only a promising youngster.

In this game Alekhine's opponent apparently approached his task in a condescending frame of mind. Eventually the position of Diagram 67 was reached. White has two bishops against bishop and knight, which is generally considered a positional advantage. However, he wants to force the exchange of his remaining knight for Black's remaining bishop. This, he reasons rather academically, will give him two bishops against two knights – an overwhelming advantage.

Alapin - Alekhine
Carlsbad 1911

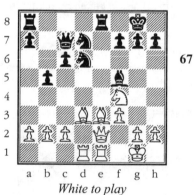

67

White to play

So White proceeds with a forced combination that he is confident will achieve his objective.

1.g4?!

This pawn thrust seriously weakens White's castled position. It is therefore a move that no player of master strength would make lightly. Nevertheless, Alapin does make it because he expects to gain a compensating advantage.

What is his reasoning?

He sees that if Black's attacked bishop retreats, he can capture it with his knight, thus achieving his objective (two bishops against two knights).

On the other hand, if Black tries to avoid this line by playing 1...♗×d3, then White replies 2.♕×d3, thereby winning a piece.

Imagine Alapin's astonishment when young Alekhine plays the "impossible":

1...♗×d3!! 2.♕×d3

After 2.♕×d3

But Alapin's astonishment turns to chagrin when his apparently green adversary continues:

2...♘e5!

This is a real Alekhine combination, of the kind that the chess world came later to expect from him.

After a lengthy study of the position, Alapin beat a crestfallen retreat with 3.♕f1.

Now let us see what would have happened if he had won a piece as planned:

3.♕×d6? ♘×f3+

This is the consequence of White's weakening of his position.

4.♔f2 ♕×d6 5.♖×d6 ♘×e1 6.♖d2

Now 6.♔×e1 will not do, so White tries to trap the knight.

6...g6 7.♖e2 ♖×e3! 8.♔×e3

If now 8.♖×e3 ♘×c2 and the knight escapes, leaving Black two pawns ahead.

8...♖e8+ 9.♔d2 ♘f3+ 10.♔c3 ♖×e2 11.♘×e2 c5

And Black wins the ending.

The previous example started from a middlegame position. In practice, the opening is an even richer source of obvious and forced moves. Here is a good example, in which White is in for a shattering surprise.

Tartakower – Capablanca
New York 1924

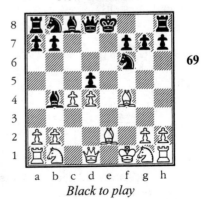

Black to play

White threatens to win a piece with 2.♗xb8 ♖xb8 3.♕a4+. Black can defend the threat easily enough by castling, but he prefers what Capa was fond of calling *une petite combinaision.* (In plain American, a little gimmick.)

1...d×c4!

A subtle defense, though it looks like a pure oversight. Tartakower goes blithely ahead with his "forced" win of a piece.

2.♗×b8 ♘d5!

The surprise! And there are still more surprises as the full meaning of this move dawns on Tartakower.

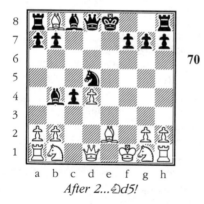

After 2...♘d5!

Black's unexpected knight move protects his exposed bishop and in addition threatens ...♘e3+, winning White's queen.

Thus White once more learns the age-old, bitter lesson: don't embark on an attack when your own king is vulnerable.

There is still another finesse involved. Tartakower may have thought that he could now play 3.♗f4 so that if 3...♘×f4? 4.♕a4+ still leaves White with a piece to the good.

But on 3...♗f4 Black has 3...♕f6!! threatening not only 4...♕×f4+ but also 4...♘e3+ because of the pin on the white bishop.

So White's forced variation was not forced at all, and he has nothing better than a crestfallen king move.

3.♔f2 ♖×b8 4.♗×c4 0-0

Black has come out of the opening with a far superior position.

The flaw in the previous, forced variation, though very pretty, was one that any first-class player should have foreseen. In the following example, Black's lapse seems almost excusable, even though he loses with a piece ahead. But then the game was played at a rapid-transit tournament, where anything can happen.

Schmid – Petrosian
Stockholm 1952

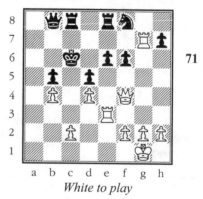

White to play

White, a piece down, has some vague attacking possibilities, as Black's king looks somewhat insecure. He has an inspiration: leaving his queen *en prise,* he works up a mating threat with:

1.♖a3!!?

So that if 1...♕×f4 2.♖a6#. A terrifying realization in a rapid-transit game!

Looking the situation over calmly, Black should be able to realize that what the position calls for is 1...♘d7!, blocking the combined action of White's rooks.

Instead, Black chooses the obvious way of guarding against ♖h6#.

1...♔b6??

Obvious? It loses by force.

White's winning method is so unbelievably subtle that even a player with plenty of time at his disposal might succumb to his brilliant trap. What is the warning that the position shrieks to Black? It is Black's *exclusive control of the seventh rank.* (Hence the recommendation of 1...♘d7! to blockade the rank.)

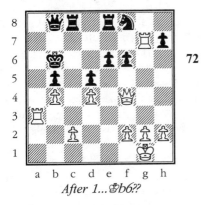

After 1...♔b6??

2.♕d6+!!

Unbelievable, but there it is.

If 2...♕×d6 3.♖ga7 and Black cannot defend himself against the coming ♖3a6#!

2...♖c6

Another obvious defense – and it won't do.

3.♕c5+!! ♖×c5 4.b×c5+ ♔c6 5.♖a6+ ♕b6 6.♖×b6#

Perhaps as you play over these telling examples you're reminded of games in which you pursued the same will-o'-the-wisp. In the formation of far-reaching plans you overlook the simple one-move tactical possibilities that are the very heart of chess. By missing these relatively simple moves, you're condemning yourself to repeated disappointment.

This is a hard fault to eliminate. It would be dishonest of me to tell you that it's easy to overcome.

So, when you're on the point of playing an "obvious" or "forced" move, make sure it's the *best* move. As Tarrasch used to say, "You must see it!"

The queer, consoling paradox is that when you concentrate on finding the strongest move in any given position, you automatically develop the power to plan and carry out long-range combinations.

It's all very well to walk with your head in the clouds. Quite enjoyable, too. But you won't enjoy it for long if in the process you trip over a rock and break your neck.

Never forget this: the most important move in any game of chess is always... the very next move.

Chapter 5

You Don't Know When to Attack – or When to Defend

If you're like most chess players, you attack because you get a kick out of it. Attacking play, for many of us, is the cream of chess.

You defend when – well, you defend when you have to. Who *wants* to defend unless forced to do so?

It all leads to a chaotic style that loses many games. For you attack when you shouldn't and get rocked back on your heels. Or, more often than not, you miss a chance for a brilliant, smashing attack.

You botch a good many games, too, because you don't like to defend. Or because you don't realize the need for defense.

What to do? There are two approaches to this problem. One, as I've indicated earlier, is to study your basic chess temperament. What you need to know above all is: what kind of a chess player am I? Am I by temperament an attacking player or a defensive player? This self-knowledge is probably more important than any technical study of the game.

The general principles that apply to one player don't necessarily apply to another. If you're aggressive, if you revel in risks, then by all means cultivate your attacking play.

But, if you want certainty, if you don't want to commit yourself, if you prefer a waiting game, if you're not sure of yourself, avoid *speculative* attacks.

In other words, know yourself – know your likes and dislikes.

When to attack

Aside from the personality angle, you lose because you don't know how to appraise a position and decide whether an attack is feasible or not. You don't know the odds in your favor, or the odds against you. In short, you play by guesswork or by prayer.

There are four key factors that should tell you when an attack is likely to succeed. If you're aggressive, a quick check of these factors will often hold you back from a futile attack. If you're naturally conservative, a review of these factors will encourage you to attack when the prospects are favorable.

Here are the factors:

(1) The defender does not control the center. This means he's out of luck if forced to defend against a strong attack. We've discussed the importance of this in an earlier chapter, so we needn't go into it here.

If the defender does control the center, think twice before starting an attack –

especially when it calls for a sacrifice of material on your part.

(2) The defender's queen is out of play. As you'll soon see, the absence of the queen almost assures the success of your attack. For that one short critical phase you're in effect a queen ahead. For that's what happens when your queen is the heart and soul of an attack, and the opposing queen is off somewhere far from the scene of conflict.

(3) Local superiority in the attacking area. Equality of forces may be academic when it comes to a question of attack and defense. If your pieces are active and your opponent's are passive, you have the jump on him. And if your pieces are concentrated in the attacking zone and his are undeveloped and scattered, it's likely you can smash through to victory before he brings up enough to the menaced area.

If the defender suffers from bad communication because you control the center, chances are he'll never bring up adequate reserves to hurl back your attack.

If in addition his queen is out of play, then, as I've stressed, your attack is likely to be overwhelming. His king will be trapped in the crossfire of your pieces.

(4) Pawn weaknesses in the defender's castled position. If any of the pawns in the defender's castled position are gone, that creates a breach for the entry of your attacking forces. If any of these pawns have been advanced, that creates a target enabling you to force open files.

Pawn weaknesses in the defender's position allow the attacking forces to infiltrate and destroy.

These four factors are not isolated. Sometimes two, or three, or even all four factors are present. But any one of them should be enough to make you pause and explore the possibilities in the position.

One last hint before we look at some practical examples. Remember this: sacrifices are delightful. They're enjoyable. We all love to make brilliant sacrifices. But they're not incomprehensible emanations of genius. When the position is ripe for them, they work with explosive force.

Some sacrifices are TNT explosions. They blast away obstacles. They cut off defending forces. They hew out a wide road for your invasion forces.

Other sacrifices are sly, full of finesse. They decoy enemy defenders. They trip up potential supporters of the beleaguered king. They block lines of communication. They create subtle possibilities of confusion.

But, whatever the nature of a sacrifice, its success or failure depends on these four key factors of attack. If the factors favor you, your sacrifices will be brilliant, inspired, successful. If the factors are against you, your sacrifices will be inept, bumbling, farcical.

Defender's Queen out of Play

Here is a position in which material is even and a draw seems foreshadowed:

Znosko-Borovsky – Duras
St. Petersburg 1909

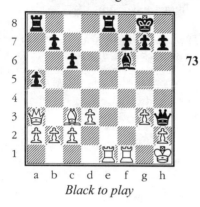

Black to play

Janowsky – Schlechter
London 1899

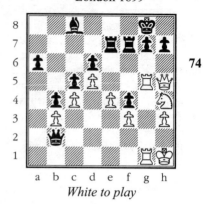

White to play

Forget about the equality of material. Actually, Black can force White to resign on the very next move.

Why? There are two reasons. The first is that White's queen is hopelessly out of play and can't get back to help guard the white king. Second reason: White has weakened his king's position by exchanging his f-pawn (opening up his second rank) and advancing his g-pawn (allowing the infiltration of Black's queen). So:

1...♖e2! Resigns

For if 2.♖xe2 ♛xf1#. And meanwhile Black threatens 2...♛g2# or 2...♛xh2#. Black's strong local superiority on the kingside tells the story.

In the next position Black is in trouble because his queen has wandered far afield to pick up a stray pawn.

White has a dangerous-looking attack, with both rooks doubled on the open g-file and his queen aggressively poised for attack.

Still, Black has defended well – apparently – by doubling his rooks on the seventh rank.

And yet White can break through brilliantly – all because Black's queen is out of the picture. Here's how it's done:

1.♛xh7+!!

If Black's queen were at f6, taking part in the defense, this sacrifice would be a miserable failure. (Why?)

1...♚xh7 2.♖h5+ ♚g8 3.♘g6 Resigns

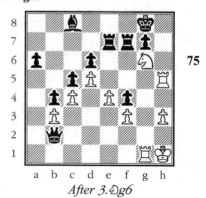

After 3.♘g6

Black is helpless – and with a (useless) queen to the good! White threatens 4.♖h8#. If 3...♖f6 4.♖h8+ ♔f7 5.♖f8#. Thus you see that Black's queen might as well be off the board!

White's local superiority on the kingside, based on the absence of Black's queen, makes the winning sacrifice possible.

Attacker's Local Superiority

This type of advantage generally does not win by itself. However, combined with another advantage (such as exploitation of pawn weaknesses in the defender's castled position), local superiority often indicates an overwhelming plus for the attacker. The following game, brief and to the point, shows how the attacker builds up local superiority of force and converts it into a winning attack.

Fuderer – Donner
Caro-Kann Defense
Beverwijk 1952

1.e4 c6 2.d4 d5 3.♘c3 d×e4 4.♘×e4 ♘f6 5.♘×f6+ e×f6 6.♗c4 ♗d6 7.♘e2 0-0 8.0-0 ♕c7 9.♘g3 ♘d7 10.♕h5!

With his last move White has achieved local superiority of force on the kingside. His queen on h5 and his bishop at c4 aim at Black's castled position. His knight and other bishop can take part very rapidly, if need be, in the prospective attack.

Black is by no means lost. But he must be alert, especially since he will be

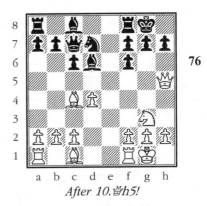

After 10.♕h5!

called upon to weaken his castled position by advancing one of his kingside pawns.

This, combined with (a) his somewhat lagging development and (b) the absence of his queen from the kingside, will soon lead to a crisis.

10...c5 11.♗d3!

Threatening 12.♕×h7# and thereby forcing Black to weaken his castled position by advancing a pawn.

11...g6

Note that 11...h6? will not do, for then the sacrifice 12.♗×h6! wins quickly: 12...g×h6 13.♕×h6 and White forces mate.

12.♕h6

With the nasty threat of 13.♘h5! (threatens 14.♕g7#) 14...g×h5 15.♕×h7#.

12...♖e8

In order to answer 13.♘h5 with 13...♗f8.

13.d×c5

67

Now Black must play 13...♗×c5, keeping his knight at d7 in order to guard his pawn at f6.

Instead, he chooses a plausible alternative, which looks much better.

13...♘×c5??

By removing the knight from contact with the kingside, he permits White's local superiority on the kingside to become overwhelming.

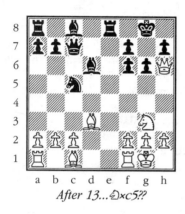

After 13...♘xc5??

14.♘h5!!

Threatening not only 15.♕g7#, but also 15.♘×f6+ followed by 16.♕×h7#. Black brought this disaster on himself by allowing White's local superiority on the kingside to become irresistible.

14...g×h5   15.♗×h7+   ♔h8
16.♗g6+ ♔g8 17.♕h7+ Resigns

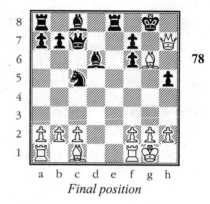

Final position

For after 17...♔f8 there follows 18.♗h6+   ♔e7   19.♕×f7+   ♔d8 20.♕×e8#.

Compare Diagram 78 with 77. After conceding local superiority on the kingside to his opponent, Black found himself in a mating net only four moves later. With his unlucky 13th move, Black was the architect of his own downfall!

In the following position, too, we can see the decisive effect of local superiority when it is applied against pawn weaknesses.

Vestol – Neu
Amsterdam Team Tournament 1954

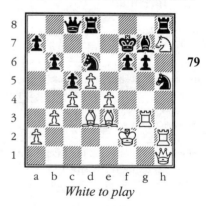

White to play

Your first thought, when you examine Diagram 79, is that White is lost because his venturesome knight is trapped.

But take a second look:

White's queen and rooks are poised for action.

Black's kingside pawn position is riddled with weaknesses.

Black's king is exposed.

Black's queen is out of play.

In other words, all the four favorable factors of successful attack are in White's hands.

1.♖×h5!

The breakthrough.

1...g×h5 2.♕×h5+ ♔g8 3.♖×g7+!

What follows is a field day for White's queen: six consecutive checks, and Black's queen can do nothing while the black king takes a lethal battering.

3...♔×g7 4.♕h6+ ♔f7 5.♕×f6+ ♔e8

Or 5...♔g8 6.♕g6#.

**6.♕×h8+ ♔f7 7.♕f6+ ♔e8
8.♕f8+ ♔d7 9.♕g7+ ♔e8
10.♘f6#**

White's violent onslaught is a perfect example of the devastating power of local superiority in carrying out an attack on a helpless king.

Defender's Pawn Weaknesses

As you've seen, your chances of attacking successfully are greatly increased if your opponent has weakened his castled king's position by advancing one of the kingside pawns. The following game illustrates this to perfection. What's more, it shows you how the defender should strive for counterattack by *counterplay in the center*.

This game also shows what happens to the defender when he fails to press his counterattack with the utmost energy and instead creates attacking lines for the enemy. You will be delighted by White's brilliant finish; but, what is more important, you will learn a great deal from White's preparations for that final attack.

Fox – Dickerson
Sicilian Defense
Brooklyn Chess Club Championship
1904

**1.e4 c5 2.♘f3 ♘c6 3.d4 c×d4
4.♘×d4 g6 5.♘c3 ♗g7**

Black has adopted the Dragon Variation, one of the most promising lines of play in this opening for the second player. It is a fighting line because it has both strong and weak points.

The strong point, of course, is that Black's fianchettoed bishop strikes at the center with terrific power. Black has won many a historic game because of the magnificent pressure exerted by this bishop.

But you have to weigh the minus factor here as well. Black has advanced his g-pawn, and if he castles kingside – which he does almost invariably – the g-pawn will be a target for White's attack.

Now you may ask yourself – or ask me – why does Black deliberately weaken himself?

A good question, but there's a convincing answer to it. In chess, every principle has worthwhile exceptions. The Dragon variation is such an exception, and for two reasons:

In the first place, chess wouldn't be the grand fighting game it is if we weren't willing to take some risk. In this case, Black is willing to subject himself to possible attack – if that's the price he has to pay for exerting strong pressure in the center.

As a corollary, let me add this thought: Black expects to keep his opponent so busy in the center that the attack on the kingside will never get going. (I'll explain this more in detail in the discussion that follows Diagram 80.)

One more important point about the Dragon Variation: Black feels he can risk weakening his kingside somewhat because his all-important dark-square bishop plays a vital defensive role at g7. The fianchettoed bishop is a big brother who is expected to guard the black king.

But (in chess there's always a "but") you have to remember that the personal qualities of the players play a big role in chess. This is particularly true here. White is a brilliant attacking player who will make the most of his attacking

chances. Black, on the other hand, is not fully aware of the needs of his position. Watch what happens because of this vast difference in attitude.

6.♗e3 d6 7.♗e2 ♘f6 8.♘b3 ♗d7 9.f4 0-0 10.g4! ♖c8 11.h4!

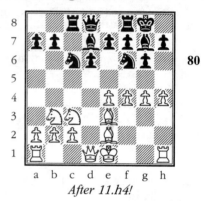

After 11.h4!

A position with fascinating possibilities. White proposes to use Black's g-pawn as a target to open a file by h4-h5 and h×g6. This will create an open file for his king rook, giving him strong local superiority on the kingside.

One thing is clear: *Black must fight back*. How? By counterattacking in the center and on the queenside, making use of his chances on the half-open c-file.

For example, 11...♘a5! 12.h5 ♘c4 with annoying counter-pressure.

Or 12.♘×a5 ♕×a5 (threatens ...♘×e4 – counterattack in the center through the action of Black's aggressive queen). If then 13.♗f3 ♗c6! renews the threat. There might follow 14.♕d3 ♘d7!. In that case Black threatens 15...♘c5, attacking the queen and also menacing ...♘×e4 or ...♘a4.

We needn't dwell on these possibilities in detail. The main point is the spirit and purpose of these powerful diversionary moves. They keep White so busy that he has no time to follow up his projected attack on the kingside.

This, then, is how *Black should have played*. Instead, there follows:

11...♔h8?

A sad loss of time.

12.g5 ♘e8 13.h5 ♗×c3+?

With this move Black negates his whole plan of the game. He removes the one piece that holds his kingside together. And remember, this same piece is the key to any counterattack. Thus, Black opens himself up to attack and at the same time deprives himself of any chance to fight back.

14.b×c3 e6 15.h×g6 f×g6

Black is lost. His kingside is bleak and undefended. He's helpless against the coming attack along the h-file. He has no counterplay in the center or on the queenside. Meanwhile White prepares to triple his heavy pieces on the open file – the highway to success.

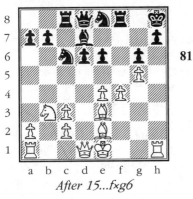

After 15...f×g6

16.♕d3 ♔g8 17.0-0-0 ♖f7 18.♖h6! ♕c7 19.♖dh1

Now that White has doubled his rooks on the h-file, he needs only one more maneuver – the transfer of his queen to that file – to make his local superiority on the kingside overwhelming.

19...♘a5 20.♗d2 ♘×b3+ 21.a×b3 b5

Here 21...♗c6 is a more promising defense, although White's pressure on the weakened pawns is too powerful.

22.♕h3

Attacking the h-pawn a third time. If Black defends that pawn by 22...♗c6 then White has 23.♕×e6.

22...♖g7 23.♖×h7 ♔f7 24.♕h6 ♗c6

Now White is ready for the final exploitation of Black's weakened pawn structure. At the same time we see sensational proof of the value of local superiority on the kingside:

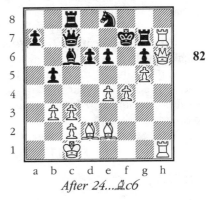

After 24...♗c6

25.♕×g6+!! ♔×g6 26.♗h5+! ♔×h7 27.♗f7 #

White's local superiority is worth far, far more that the sacrificed queen and rook. What better proof could you have that brilliant sacrifices are merely the violent explosions brought about by overwhelming local superiority?

In the following position, Black seems at first glance to have barricaded himself very cleverly. What's more, he's about to simplify by ...♖c1, whittling down the strength of White's projected attack.

Pillsbury – Showalter
Match 1897

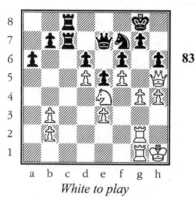

83

White to play

But White has all the trumps:

(1) Magnificently *centralized* knight which cannot be driven away.
(2) Possibility of g4-g5!!. This exploits Black's weakening of his castled position by advancing his f-pawn and h-pawn.
(3) Strong local superiority resulting from White's g4-g5!!.

1.g5!!

Smashing into the targets. Black must capture.

1...h×g5 2.h×g5 ♘×g5

Now Black hopes for 3.♘×g5 f×g5 4.♖×g5 ♖c1! and White's attack has lost all its punch. But White keeps his valuable knight.

3.♖×g5! f×g5 4.♘×g5

Threatening 5.♕h7+ and 6.♕h8#. Thus White's local superiority, together with Black's pawn weaknesses, gives White a winning attack.

4...g6 5.♕×g6+ ♕g7 6.♕e6+!

84

After 6.♕e6+!

6...♔h8

A delightful demonstration of the knight's power: if 6...♔f8 7.♕×c8+! ♖×c8 8.♘e6+ and White will be a piece to the good!

7.♖g3! ♖c1+ 8.♔g2 ♖8c2+ 9.♔f3 ♖f1+ 10.♔e4

White's king is handsomely centralized against further molesting checks, and now White menaces 11.♖h3+.

10...♖h1 11.♕e8+ Resigns

White forces mate in two.

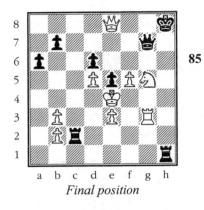

Final position

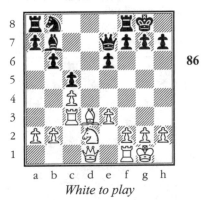

Marshall – Capablanca
Berlin 1928

White to play

By taking advantage of Black's compromising pawn moves, White swept away all valid defense on the kingside. The result was a field day for White, thanks to his crushing local superiority on the kingside.

But suppose these factors are not present?

Suppose you don't have local superiority? Suppose your opponent hasn't created a pawn target? Suppose his queen isn't out of play? Suppose he has adequate control of the center?

The answer is simple: then don't attack!

When Not to Attack

To know when to refrain from attacking when conditions are unfavorable is as much an art as carrying out a crushing attack under favorable conditions.

The art of refraining was psychologically repugnant to a great attacking player like Marshall. He always knew *how* to attack, but frequently not *when*. Take the following, for example.

White can attack with queen and bishop; but that hardly constitutes local superiority.

He can bring his queen rook to the kingside by playing e3-e4; but this would block his bishop's diagonal. Self-blocking and mutual interference can't make us very optimistic about White's attacking prospects.

As for Black, his undeveloped knight can come into play quickly, thanks to White's optimistic attacking maneuvers.

Finally, as you will see, Black can counterattack effectively in the center.

Our conclusion: White should play it safe and consolidate his position with 1.♕e2 followed by ♖d1. But you can't give such sensible advice to a fiery attacking player. So:

1.♕h5

Threatens mate.

1...h6

Ends the mate threat. Is this pawn move weakening? Doubtless – but how is White to prove that?

2.f4 ♘d7 3.e4 e5!

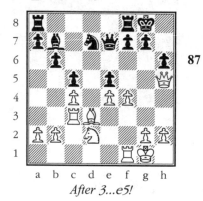

After 3...e5!

Capa's timing is flawless. If now 4.f5 ♘f6. White's queen is driven off and his bishop is buried alive. No attack here.

Or if 4.fxe5 ♘xe5 and Black's knight has an "eternal" square in the center with a lasting attack on White's isolated e-pawn, plus domination of the open d-file. In that case White has no attack worth mentioning, and Black's monopoly of the center decides easily in his favor.

4.♘f3 ♖ae8 5.♘h4 exf4!

Uncovering White's fatal weakness: the isolated e-pawn.

6.♖xf4 ♕g5!

Forcing another retreat, as exchanging queens will cost White a piece.

7.♕f3 ♘e5!

Who's attacking now? Black wins the weak pawn.

8.♕f2 ♘xd3 9.♖xd3 ♖xe4 and wins

White resigned 12 moves later. A classic example of how to hurl back an inadequate attack.

In the next example the refutation depends on a tactical finesse:

Smook – Pomar
Hollywood 1955

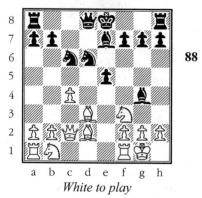

White to play

White has played many pawn moves. He lacks development; his hold on the center is feeble; he is menaced with ...♗xf3, breaking up his castled pawn position and preparing for ...♘d4 – a powerful advance in the center for Black.

This situation calls for some careful defensive measure such as 1.♗e3 (neutralizing a possible ...♘d4), or 1.♗e2 (avoiding the breakup of his pawns).

Instead, what does White think of? He thinks of attack!

1.c5?

He's influenced by a tactical finesse: 1...♗xf3 2.cxd6 wins a piece.

1...♗×f3!!

Well played.

2.c×d6 ♘d4!

Black can afford to lose a piece: he banks on White's broken kingside.

3.d×e7 ♛d7!

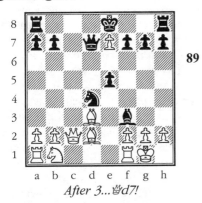

After 3...♛d7!

Now White sees that if he stops to save his queen Black has 4...♛g4 5.g3 ♛h3 and mate follows.

So he tries to win the piece in a different way:

4.♗f5 ♘×f5 5.g×f3 ♘d4

Control of the center must tell!

6.♛e4 ♛h3!

Now Black's local superiority on the kingside plus White's fatal pawn weakness completely override White's piece plus.

7.♗f4 ♘×f3+ Resigns

For if 8.♔h1 ♛×f1#. So White must give up his queen to stop mate.

When to Defend

As you well know from your own experience, we all like to attack and hate to defend. The player who has conquered his reluctance to defend will win many valuable points – and half-points!

One of the most useful – and little-known – aspects of defense is that centralization will often work wonders for the defense. See here how it accomplishes miracles:

Ulvestad – Reinfeld
Ventnor City 1939

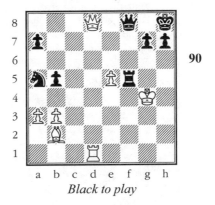

Black to play

Black has only a split second to make his last move to come within the time control (40 moves in the first two hours).

He sees that:
(1) His knight is attacked
(2) He can't play 1...♛×d8?? for then 2.♖×d8+ forces mate.
(3) He has a draw with 1...♖f4+, for example 2.♔g3 ♖f3+ 3.♔g2 ♖f2+ 4.♔g1 ♖f1+!.

But, after all, he reasons, he's a pawn ahead. Why not get in one more move and then, with plenty of time available, he can look around for some resource to save the game.

1...h5+!? 2.♔h4!

Now Black is still in trouble. He has removed the mate threat, to be sure, but after 2...♛xd8+? 3.♖xd8+ ♔h7 4.e6 White must win.

Nor does Black have a perpetual check any longer, for if 2...♖f4+ 3.♔xh5! ♖f5+ 4.♔g6! and wins. What to do?

After studying the position for over a half hour, Black gets the right idea: he must centralize!

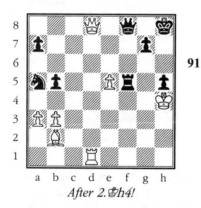

After 2.♔h4!

2...♔g8!

First point: Black will use his king to stop the dangerous passed pawn.

Second point: if White plays 3.♕xa5?? his queen will be out of play, giving Black local superiority on the kingside: 3...♖f4+ 4.♔g3 ♖g4+ or 4.♔h3 ♕f5+. In either case Black forces mate.

3.e6

Apparently deadly, but Black has an easy defense by centralizing his knight.

3...♘c6! 4.♕xf8+ ♔xf8 5.♖d7 ♔e8! 6.♖xg7 ♘d8! 7.♖xa7 ♘xe6 Drawn

Black saved the game by his timely centralization!

So, as you can see, knowing when to defend is a very useful art. Accurate timing of the defense is particularly important in such openings as the King's Gambit, where White announces his aggressive intentions at the very start of the game. Ordinarily Black is so flustered by this frank hostility that he caves in rather spinelessly. (We see an example of that in the Rudolph-Amateur game on page 45.)

But here our newly gained knowledge can be of great help to us. When White plays the King's Gambit, he's not in possession of the four key factors needed for a successful attack.

This knowledge should hearten you when playing the defense. You can succeed in defending yourself against the King's Gambit if you realize that the odds are in your favor. In other words, seize the counterattack – as Black does in the following game.

It doesn't take Black long to realize that *counterpressure in the center* is his only chance. Consequently, he develops his pieces rapidly, getting his king out of harm's way at the same time. Once Black has made his crucial decision, he carries it out incisively, not bothering to defend the gambit pawn. A good example for you to follow!

Kieninger – Eliskases
King's Gambit
Stuttgart 1939

**1.e4 e5 2.f4 exf4 3.♘f3 ♘f6!
4.♘c3 d5! 5.exd5 ♘xd5 6.♘xd5
♛xd5 7.d4 ♝e7!**

Indirectly defending the gambit pawn, as White is threatening 8.♗xf4 ♛e4+ 9.♛e2!.

8.c4 ♛e4+ 9.♔f2 ♝f5 10.c5!?

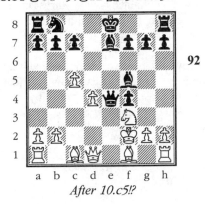

After 10.c5!?

Black's queen is powerfully centralized, and yet the position of his king and queen on the same (open) file is disquieting. Black's king must vamoose.

10...♘c6!

Admirable counterattack. Black develops a piece; takes the sting out of ♗b5+ followed by ♖e1; and brings pressure to bear on the d-pawn.

11.♗b5

In order to harass Black with ♖e1.

11...♛d5!

Still maintaining a strongly centralized position for his queen. Black discreetly renounces his extra pawn in order to get off the "hot" file.

**12.♗xf4 0-0-0! 13.♗e3 ♝f6!
14.♛a4 ♝e4!**

The crisis. Instead of protecting his a-pawn, Black counterattacks by knocking out one of the props (White's knight) of the d-pawn.

After 14...♝e4!

In effect Black is offering the sacrifice of a rook in order to press his counterattack in the center: 15.♗xc6 ♛xc6 16.♛xa7 ♝xf3 17.gxf3 ♝xd4 18.♗xd4 ♖xd4 19.♛a8+ ♔d7 20.♛xh8 ♛xc5! and White is lost.

Here is a typical possibility: 21.♖ac1 ♖d2+ 22.♔g3 ♛g5+ 23.♔h3 ♛g2+ 24.♔h4 ♖d4+ 25.♔h5 ♛g6#!. And why is all this possible? Because White, in snapping up the rook in this hypothetical variation, puts his queen out of play.

So, back to Diagram 93 for the actual continuation:

15.♗xc6 ♛xc6 16.♛xc6 ♝xc6

Black has beaten off the attack, and he is still stalking the d-pawn!

With the queen removed from the board, whatever attacking possibilities White may have had are now gone. Black's pressure on the d-pawn is stronger than ever, and he has nothing to fear from White. Magnificent counterplay by Black has given him all the trumps.

17.♖ad1 ♖he8 18.♖he1 ♗×f3! 19.♔×f3 ♗×d4! 20.♗×d4 ♖×e1 21.♖×e1 ♖×d4

Black's tenacity has been rewarded. Thanks to his splendid timing of his counterattack, he has won a pawn and steered safely into the endgame.

By now you have a good insight into the nature of attack and defense. You've learned that if certain landmarks are absent, your attack will fail miserably.

You've learned that your sacrifices won't yield pay dirt if the proper basis for an attack is missing.

You've also seen that an inadequately prepared attack is one of the surest ways for you to lose a game.

And – equally important – you've seen how a determined counter-thrust in the center can knock your attack into a cocked hat.

Above all, you've learned something about timing. You can now see that you've lost many a game by not knowing when to attack or when to defend.

Chapter 6

You Lose Because You Ignore the Odds

If I were asked to give the one reason above all why you lose at chess, I'd say it's because you underestimate the importance of the endgame.

And this in face of the fact that certainly over 60 per cent of all games of chess are decided in the endgame stage. If you're going to ignore endgames, you're giving odds of three to two that you'll invariably lose.

Simple, isn't it?

Why do you ignore this important feature of chess? Because endgames bore you to death.

My purpose is not to teach you how to play endgames. What I want to do is to point out the reasons why you lose at chess. And, as I've indicated, the principal reason you lose is that you ignore endgames, deliberately evade them – they just don't interest you.

What I hope to do here, then, is to modify your dogmatic and unprofitable attitude by showing you that endgame play is not only important, it's also beautiful and exciting.

To be perfectly frank about it, I want to sell you the idea that you ought to cultivate your endgame skill and thereby eliminate one of the chief reasons you lose at chess. Examine the games of any noted master and you will find that first-class endgame play accounts for a substantial part of his success. This can also be true of your own games.

What Is an Endgame?

Perhaps you're not too clear as to just what an endgame is.

You're doubtless familiar with composed endings. These are not from actual play; they're artificially constructed positions in which one side can win or draw in a very ingenious, seemingly impossible, manner.

In such a composed ending, every unit on the board has been placed there for a special – functional – reason. There's no superfluous or useless material on the board.

But in endgames that we meet in practical play, the situation is by no means so clear. *It's up to you* to bring order out of apparent chaos, to make your pieces and pawns work for you. If you don't know how to go about it, you lose.

An endgame position, the kind we meet in practical play, is one which has been simplified to some extent by prior exchanges. *In almost all cases the queens have disappeared.*

There are many kinds of endings – those in which each player has only his king and one or more pawns. (In some cases, one of the players has no pawn at all.)

Then there are rook-and-pawn endings – the most common type – in which each player has a king, a rook, and some pawns. (And in these and other types of endings, it may be that one player has some pawns, while his opponent hasn't any at all.) Endings with two rooks on each side are comparatively rare.

Another type is the minor-piece ending, in which a bishop or knight is opposed by a bishop or knight, with some pawns still left on the board.

In a few instances we have queen and pawn endings, where the queens have not been exchanged, to be sure, but all the other pieces have.

So there you have the general picture: an endgame position is one in which some pieces – generally the queens – have been exchanged. In any case, considerable simplification has taken place.

Why do you avoid endgames? Because you avoid the exchange of queens. As you see it, once the queens are gone, all the fun disappears from the game of chess. The fact is, you don't know what most endgames are about, and you don't know how to win them.

While you're sputtering with indignation, may I tell you something about my own experience?

When I was a youngster I hated endgames – just as you do. My head was stuffed with all the stale clichés about endgames. You know: "Endgames are

boring." "Nothing ever happens." "Too simple." I wanted action!

When an endgame loomed, I avoided it at all cost by the simple expedient of stupidly seeking a lost game. Once in a while I allowed myself to be dragged into an ending; but, since I hated and feared it, how could I play it well?

After a while I began to improve slowly and started to take a grudging interest in endings. But even at that stage I'd ask myself: how was it that the great tacticians whom I worshiped – men like Morphy, Chigorin, Pillsbury, Alekhine – were marvelous endgame players? How could they stand these dreary endings?

In my innocence and ignorance I failed to realize that tacticians make wonderful endgame players because all endings are decided by *tactical* means. After all, how else could they be decided? No matter how subtle and strategical an ending may be, it is won or lost in the last analysis by some *tactical* point: a mating threat, an unforeseen capture, a pin or a fork, a double attack, a pawn promotion, etc.

And then, consider this: the very essence of almost all endings is *the queening of a pawn*. This in itself is one of the strongest, most violent, most decisive moves in the game of chess. It explains why the advantage of a pawn has caused the world championship to change hands. Once you realize this, your interest in endgames is bound to be aroused.

And here's another point. The exchange of queens doesn't by any means kill the lively possibilities in a game of chess. When the queens disappear, the other pieces take on added importance and power. If you're alert to your opportunities and appreciative of that delicate power, you can achieve some entrancing conclusions.

Mating Attacks in the Endgame

You'd truly be surprised, for example, if you could realize how often mating attacks turn up in endgame play. Here's a beauty:

Kmoch - Schelfhout
Amsterdam 1934

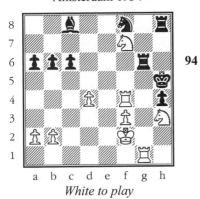

White to play

White mates by:

1.罝f5+‼

A beautiful move!

1...♗×f5 2.♘f4#!

Thus White's first move was a clearance maneuver to make room for the checkmating knight.

As you would expect, the great tactician Marshall brought off some magnificent strokes in endgame play. Here's an example showing how he whips up a splendid mating finish out of a position which doesn't look too interesting:

Esser – Marshall
London 1899

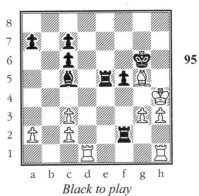

Black to play

Most players would be content to continue 1...罝×c2, regaining the pawn and forcing the win of another pawn. But Marshall sees a much more forcing line:

1...罝f4+‼ Resigns

Thunderstruck, White at last realizes that 2.g×f4 allows 2...♗f2# while if 2.♗×f4 ♗e7+ and mate next move.

Who said that endgames are dull? Just for good measure, see what happens to the great Alekhine.

Petrov – Alekhine
Margate 1938

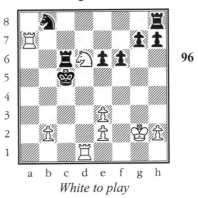

White to play

White can win a pawn by playing 1.♘e4+ and 2.♖×g7, but that would be the work of a butcher. Instead, White plays like a great artist:

1.b4+!! ♔×b4

Black's king must walk the plank. If 1...♔b6 2.♖b7+ ♔a6 3.♖a1#! So you don't need the queen to force checkmate!

2.♖b7+ ♔c3

Or 2...♔c5 3.♖b5#. White's pieces know no mercy.

3.♘e4+ ♔c2

If 3...♔c4 4.♖d4#.

4.♖bb1! Resigns

After 4.♖bb1!

Even if Black stands on his head, he can't ward off 5.♖dc1#. Exquisite play!

Granted, you may admit unwillingly, but not all endgames are this fascinating. True, but neither are all middlegames full of brilliant sacrifices.

Brilliant Sacrifices in the Endgame

Even without mating attacks there is still considerable scope for sparkling

endgame play. Nimzovich, that master of the bizarre and the fantastic, shows us what a player of imagination can accomplish in a position that looks hopelessly blocked:

Amateur – Nimzovich
Lund 1921

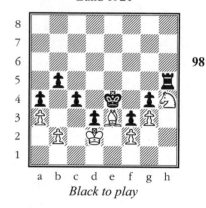

98

Black to play

Here is how Nimzovich smashes open the position:

1...b4!!

You won't be able to appreciate this move until you reach the point where White resigns. Meanwhile, note that Black threatens 2...c3+ 3.b×c3 b×a3, winning by the text method.

2.a×b4 ♖×h4!!

Typical Nimzovich. First he attacks on one wing, then on the other. Each individual move looks nonsensical, but both moves add up to a brilliant plan.

3.g×h4 g3!!

Is Black playing giveaway chess? One present after another! But observe that he threatens to *queen a pawn* by ...g2.

By relentlessly operating on both wings, Nimzovich gradually reduces his opponent to helplessness. The queening of a black pawn is only a matter of time.

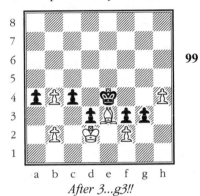

99

After 3...g3!!

4.f×g3 c3+!!

Slyly taking advantage of the fact that White's bishop no longer has pawn protection. Consequently, if now 5.♔×c3 ♔×e3 and Black queens a pawn.

5.b×c3 a3! Resigns

For if 6.♔c1 (to stop the a-pawn from queening), 6...♔×e3 and Black must queen a pawn.

Brilliant as Black's play is in this example, it is dwarfed by what happens in the next position:

Ortueta – Sanz
Madrid 1934

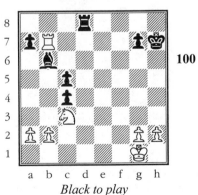

100

Black to play

"Even in material, queens off the board, draw."

That's what you think. Watch what happens:

1...♖d2 2.♘a4

Naturally.

2...♖×b2!!

A superb sacrifice, played to force the queening of a pawn.

3.♘×b2 c3

Threatening 4...c×b2 and 5...b1♕+.

If White tries 4.♘d3, then 4...c4+ 5.♖×b6 c×d3! and Black queens one of his pawns.

4.♖×b6!

Expecting 4...a×b6 5.♘d3 c4 6.♘c1 and White wins with his piece ahead.

101

After 4.♖×b6!

4...c4!!!

The finest move of the ending. He prevents ♘d3, and thereby threatens to queen by advancing ...c2, etc.

5.♖b4!

White makes a good fight of it. On 5...c×b2 6.♖×b2 wins easily. And if 5...c2 6.♖×c4 with two pieces to the good.

5...a5!!

This long-foreseen resource crushes White despite his two pieces to the good. For if now 6.♖×c4 c×b2 and Black queens. Likewise, if 6.♖b7 c2 and again Black queens.

6.♘a4 a×b4! Resigns

White's extra knight is purely ornamental: there's no way to prevent Black from queening a pawn.

In both these very lovely endings you saw that all the brilliant play centered about the queening of a pawn. Do such endings always *have* to be brilliant? Not at all. I merely used the brilliancy as a sugarcoated pill to hold your interest. Without the bait of a brilliancy, you might have growled at the idea of admiring an ending.

Queening a Pawn

By now perhaps you're at least a partly converted sinner. Maybe you're willing to look at a run-of-the-mill ending in which one of the players is poised to queen a pawn. No brilliancy here; but I think you'll enjoy White's procedure.

Morphy – Salmon
Blindfold Exhibition
Birmingham 1858

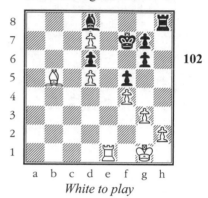

102

White to play

Morphy, who rarely missed a trick in endgame play, immediately seizes his chance:

1.♖e8! Now Black can't very well let himself in for 1...♖×e8?? 2.d×e8♕+ and wins, as the new queen is protected by the white bishop. **1...♖f8 2.♔f2!**

White's king is headed for c8, and there isn't a thing Black can do about it!

2...g5 3.♔e3! g4 4.♔d3! g5 5.♗c6! g×f4 6.g×f4 ♖g8 7.♔c4! ♖f8 8.♔b5! ♖g8 9.♔a6! ♖f8 10.♔b7! ♖g8 11.♔c8!

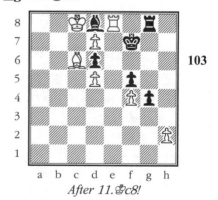

103

After 11.♔c8!

White has carried out his plan and now wins a piece by forcing the queening of his far-advanced passed pawn.

11...♗b6 12.♖×g8 ♔×g8 13.d8♕+ Resigns

Perhaps, to your surprise, you found this ending enjoyable, despite the lack of brilliance. Logic has a charm all its own, and even a brilliant combination is nothing more than window dressing for a logical idea.

In the previous example the logic of White's winning process was fairly obvious. In the following position the winning idea is equally logical but not so easy to find.

Unzicker – Lundin
Amsterdam Team Tournament 1954

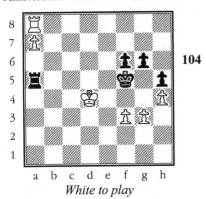

104

White to play

Here are the basic elements of the situation:

White's passed pawn is on the seventh rank, ready to queen.

Unfortunately, White's rook can't move, as this would lose the precious passed pawn.

Black's rook prevents the pawn from queening; but, by the same token, the black rook is tied down to the a-file.

Now what about the kings?

Black's king is rooted to the spot, for if the king moves, White plays ♖e8+ and queens his pawn safely.

White's king has freedom of action, and *this is the key to the win.* White's king is to head for h6. Then – but let's wait till White's king arrives.

1.♔c4 ♖a6

Note that 1...g5 won't do, for after 2.h×g5 Black can't recapture without exposing his king to a fatal rook check!

2.♔c5 ♖a1 3.♔d6 ♖a3 4.♔e7 ♖a6

And not 4...♖×f3, for then White moves his rook and queens his passed pawn.

5.♔f7 ♖a3 6.♔g7 ♖a1 7.♔h6 ♖a6

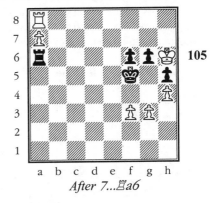

105

After 7...♖a6

Now that White's king has arrived at h6, he can safely give up his passed pawn, getting two hostile pawns in return.

**8.罝b8! 罝×a7 9.罝b5+ 含e6
10.含×g6 罝a8 11.含×h5 罝g8 12.g4
罝h8+ 13.含g6 Resigns**

Black realizes that the situation is
hopeless. After 13...罝×h4 14.罝b6+ he
remains two pawns down, powerless
against their advance to the queening
row.

King and Pawn Endings

In this type of ending, in which only
kings and pawns are left on the board,
there is just one way to win: by
queening a pawn. (Of course, once in a
great while, a freak checkmate may turn
up.)

There is therefore an enormous
disproportion between the low power
output of the kings and the tremendous
value of the prospective queen. When
you look at these endings, the pawns are
just pawns to you. But not to the master!
To him, these lowly pawns are *potential
queens* – with all the dynamic power of
that mighty piece. That's why these
endings are always exciting and full of
delicate manipulation. For example:

Keres – Alekhine
Dresden 1936

106

Black to play

Black is a pawn ahead and has two
passed pawns. Meanwhile he has to
keep his eye – or so it seems – on
White's passed pawn.

Black has two winning lines. True to his
temperament, Alekhine chooses the
more daring method:

1...含g4!

Allowing White's passed pawn to
queen!

2.d6 g2 3.含f2 含h3

If now 4.含g1 e3 5.d7 e2 6.d8豆 e1豆#!.
If instead 6.含f2 in this variation, there
follows 6...g1豆+ 7.含×g1 e1豆#!.

4.d7 e3+!

If now 5.含e2 g1豆 6.d8豆 豆f2+ and
White must choose between 7.含d3
豆d2+ when he loses his queen, and
7.含d1 e2+ when Black gets a new
queen. Of course, if 5.含×e3, Black
queens with check.

107

After 4...e3+!

**5.含f3 g1豆 6.d8豆 豆f2+ 7.含e4 e2
8.豆d7+ 含g2 9.豆g4+ 含f1 Resigns**

White's checks are exhausted, for if
10.豆h3+ 豆g2+! forcing the exchange

of queens and the queening of the passed pawn.

Now you would think that all these beautiful possibilities do a great deal of honor to this "simple" king and pawn ending. But there's more to it, and for this reason: Alekhine's winning method is too daring to recommend it to the rest of us.

Actually there's a much more systematic method, so let's go back to Diagram 106 and see how the alternative line goes:

1...♔e5! 2.♔e2 ♔d6 3.♔e3 ♔c7!

Black can afford to leave his e-pawn unguarded, for after 4.♔xe4?? g2 the g-pawn queens by force.

4.♔e2 ♔b7

Note that Black's king remains within range of White's passed pawn.

5.♔e3

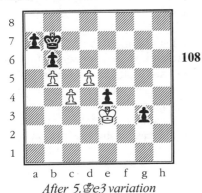

After 5.♔e3 variation

5...a5!

Getting a third passed pawn, which White must liquidate at once, for his king can't catch three free pawns.

6.bxa6+ ♔xa6

Black's king can still stop the pawn from queening.

7.♔e2 ♔b7 8.♔e3 ♔c7 9.♔e2 ♔d6 10.♔e3

Now that Black has swung his king back, what has he accomplished? This:

10...b5!!

By splitting White's pawns, he liquidates White's passed pawn. Very fine play!

11.cxb5 ♔xd5

Black now plays ...♔c5 followed by ...♔xb5. Then, with two passed pawns ahead, he has an easy win. All he has to do is to bring his king in to support the advance of the pawns.

From this one ending you can get a good idea of the richness of possibilities in these "simple" king and pawn endings.

Now that you've seen how pawn promotion can play a vital role in the ending, let's look at one last motif which is common to many types of endgames.

Zugzwang, or the Squeeze Play

Zugzwang is a German word meaning "move-compulsion." It refers to positions in which a player has all his forces protected, but must lose some of that protection because it's his turn to move. To force your opponent into *Zugzwang* is to subject him to a squeeze play that wins the game. Here's how it's done:

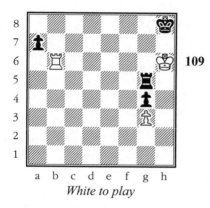

White to play

109

If 1.♔xg5 axb6 and the game will end in a draw. And if 1.♖b8+ ♖g8 and Black is safe. But White has a squeeze play with:

1.♖b7!!

Black is lost!

Thus, if 1...♖g8 2.♖h7#.

And if the black rook moves off the g-file, White forces mate with 2.♖b8+ etc.

Here's another squeeze play:

Kupferstich – Andreassen
Junior World Championship 1953

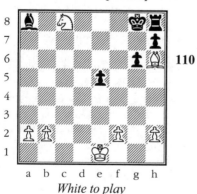

110

White to play

1.♘d6!!

Black is in *Zugzwang*. He can't move his king or rook, and bishop moves won't help against White's plan: bringing his king to e7, after which White plays ♘e4 (or ♘e8) followed by ♘f6#! Although this plan takes ten moves to execute, it's absolutely forced. Hence Black resigns.

I hope I've convinced you that endgames needn't be dull – that they can be beautiful and exciting. What could be more logical than Unzicker's win in Diagram 104, or more brilliant than Nimzovich's breakthrough in Diagram 98? Have you ever seen a more striking middlegame mate than Marshall's amazing line in Diagram 95? What could be more elegant than the beautiful sacrifices produced from Diagram 100?

But, as you've now seen, endgames are not only beautiful, they're vitally important. For neglecting the endgame is one of the principal reasons you lose at chess.

So, don't be afraid to exchange queens, especially if your opponent is an aggressive, attacking player who is eager to keep the queens on the board. By avoiding the exchange of queens in such situations, you're creating a twofold reason why you lose at chess!

Chapter 7

You Lose Because You Play the Board – and Not the Man

Another way of stating it: you lose because your play is too inflexible. You play in a rigid and mechanical manner.

The trouble is that you've learned from chess books that there is *a* right way to play. Remember that the object of a chess book is to teach you to play sound chess against an impersonal opponent who's presumed to be infallible or mighty close to it. That's okay for a book of instruction, but it's not very helpful when you play a real, live opponent. For your opponents are far from infallible. They're not automatons; they're human beings. There's such a thing as being too careful, too subtle, too much of a perfectionist. Then what? You're careful to avoid an isolated pawn – and you walk into a checkmate. You develop your pieces faultlessly – and overlook the fact that your opponent has left his queen *en prise*.

Don't get me wrong. You *can* learn a lot from chess books. But one thing you'll never learn from them is the knack of how to concentrate on your opponent's strong and weak points.

If you don't have that knack, you lose many a game you might have won because you don't exploit your opportunities. If only you'd known the secret of winning such games – by channeling them into paths where your opponent is most vulnerable.

So, take this advice: avoid those lines of play where your opponent is at his best. Aim for lines of play where he's weakest. In short, play the man – and not the board.

Playing the man and not the board

Does this sound too Machiavellian? Well, here's how Morphy did it:

Just to make it more drastic, Morphy is giving the odds of queen rook. So, remove this piece from the white side before you start the game.

Morphy – Amateur
Two Knights' Defense
New Orleans 1855

1.e4 e5 2.♘f3 ♘c6 3.♗c4 ♘f6 4.♘g5

Very significant. As a rule, Morphy avoided repeated opening moves with the same piece. But here he's playing a duffer, and he knows he can take liberties. (Naturally you can only afford to take liberties against weak players. You're playing the man, not the board.)

4...d5 5.e×d5

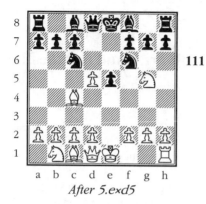

After 5.exd5

Now, if Black were a good player –
which he isn't – he would play 5...♘a5,
happy that the diagonal of White's
dangerous light-square bishop is closed.

But Black doesn't play 5...♘a5 – just
as Morphy knew he wouldn't.

The amateur's trouble is that he doesn't
know what he's up against;
consequently he doesn't take the proper
measures to avoid trouble or else to
counterattack smartly. The result is
inevitably disaster.

5...♘×d5

This move is perfectly sound – *but not
against Morphy!* If you analyzed this
position for six million years, it would
always be a win for Black – but not in
this particular game.

6.♘×f7?!

The famous "Fried Liver" Attack. It
wouldn't be sound even if Morphy had
his queen rook; imagine, then, how
unsound it must be without the queen
rook. But again, remember that Morphy
is playing the man and not the board.

6...♔×f7 7.♕f3+ ♔e6

Morphy now has the kind of position he
wanted: the black king is out in the open
and Black sees ghosts all over the place.
Terrified and confused, he's too
befuddled to brush off Morphy's attack,
which is mostly sham and show.

8.♘c3

Black should now defend his pinned
knight by 8...♘ce7 followed by ...c6.
With a solid position and two pieces to
the good, he'd have an easily won
game. Instead, badly rattled by the pin,
Black allows himself to be led astray by
Morphy's menacing moves.

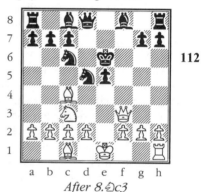

After 8.♘c3

8...♘d4

Losing back one of his pieces
without compensation. Still, this is a
luxury that Black can afford.

9.♗×d5+ ♔d6 10.♕f7!

A bit of Morphy; he threatens
11.♘e4#!

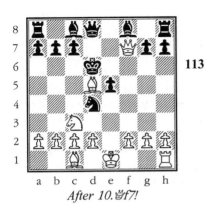

After 10.♕f7!

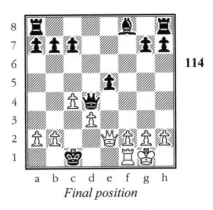

Final position

Now Black can throttle the attack – as Morphy well knows – with 10...♕e7!. But Black is asleep at the switch. Worse yet, he's snoring with all stops open.

10...♗e6? 11.♗×e6 ♘×e6 12.♘e4+ ♚d5 13.c4+! ♚×e4 14.♕×e6

Morphy has done a wonderful job of addling Black's wits, so Black misses 14...♚d4!, which would still give him a playable defense.

14...♕d4?

Now Morphy wins by force. His diabolical tactics have worked.

15.♕g4+ ♚d3 16.♕e2+ ♚c2

The compulsory king march leads to a droll finish.

17.d3+ ♚×c1

Less spectacular, but basically no better is 17...♚b1 18.0-0 ♚×a2 19.♕c2 and the coming discovered check crushes Black.

18.0-0#!

Let's sum up what happened here, for it points out an important moral. White started the game a rook down – a hopeless material disadvantage. That is, *it would be hopeless if the players were evenly matched*. But they aren't evenly matched. White is by far the better player – so much so that his being a rook down hardly matters.

Note this too. By paying attention to conventional ideas of soundness White would get nowhere. *He must play the man* – confuse him, befuddle him, overwhelm him.

This game, I admit, is rather drastic. But it's not exaggerated. It's a faithful picture of the success that's in for you if you have an accurate notion of your opponent's weaknesses and know how to exploit them.

Bamboozling a World Champion

No player is free from weaknesses – no, not even a world champion. And here's the proof:

Wilhelm Steinitz was one of the three greatest chess masters of all time. (I rank him with Lasker and Alekhine.)

In his younger years Steinitz was a ferocious gambiteer. From the very start he burned with eagerness to rid himself of pawns and pieces in order to win brilliantly.

Later on, with all the zeal of a converted sinner, Steinitz claimed that material advantage must always win – any time and every time. When he was a pawn to the good, he was dogmatically certain that he *had* to win. It was all one to him whether his opponent was Zukertort or Chigorin or a little girl in pigtails.

In short, Steinitz played the board and not the man. Because Steinitz was a superman himself, he often got away with this weird theory of his – that it doesn't matter who your opponent is, so long as the objective position favors you.

Well, eventually a new crop of chess masters appeared, and their idea was, play the *man*, not the board. They noticed that when Steinitz played against the Evans Gambit he tied himself in knots. So they played Evans Gambits against him, even in world championship matches. Here's how one of these extraordinary games went:

Gunsberg – Steinitz
Evans Gambit
World Championship Match 1891

1.e4 e5 2.♘f3 ♘c6 3.♗c4 ♗c5

There is an interesting eyewitness account of this game: "'I wish Gunsberg would play an Evans Gambit,' said a spectator, but from the tome in which he uttered it he evidently considered it a hopeless and forlorn wish. The two masters had just then ascended to the room to play on the floor above. The first three moves were sent down rapidly, and the despondent one began, figuratively speaking, to prick up his ears. When the fourth move came down, he uttered an exclamation of delight, for at last the desire of many was realized, and an Evans Gambit formed the subject of battle."

Here's the reason for the excitement. Steinitz was at that time contesting a cable match with Chigorin and playing an incredibly outlandish defense against the Evans. The spectators at the present game, in the spirit of Romans witnessing gladiatorial combats, were hoping that Steinitz would be foolish enough to handicap himself with the same distasteful defense.

4.b4

If Steinitz were playing the man and not the board, it would be the simplest thing in the world to play 4...♗b6, grievously upsetting his opponent by confronting him with an unexpected problem.

But nothing of the sort: Steinitz can win a pawn, and "therefore the game." So he takes:

4...♗×b4 5.c3 ♗a5 6.0-0 ♕f6?

What's the use of writing chess books if even world champions are going to violate the most elementary principles of strategy by prematurely developing the queen? But Steinitz considers that no hardship is too great when he's a pawn up.

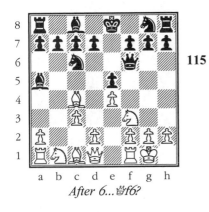

After 6...♕f6?

7.d4 ♘h6 8.♗g5 ♕d6 9.d5

He blocks his light-square bishop's diagonal, but by way of compensation he condemns Black's knight to inactivity. Note, by the way, that Gunsberg is following Chigorin move for move, craftily egging Steinitz on to further disastrous eccentricities.

9...♘d8 10.♕a4! ♗b6 11.♘a3!

The knight is to come into the game very powerfully with ♘c4 later on.

11...c6

Black is stifling – but he still clutches his pawn.

12.♗e2!

A fantastic situation. Merely by exploiting his opponent's stubbornness, White is building up a magnificent position.

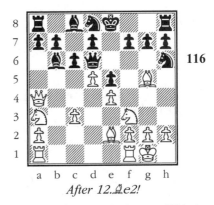

After 12.♗e2!

If Black tries 12...cxd5 then 13.♖fd1 is much in White's favor.

At this point White threatens 13.♘c4 ♕c7 (forced) 14.d6 ♕b8, and Black is buried alive. White's game practically plays itself.

12...♗c7 13.♘c4 ♕f8

And Steinitz is still well content with his position!

14.d6! ♗xd6 15.♘b6 ♖b8 16.♕xa7

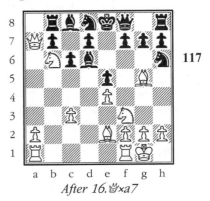

After 16.♕xa7

This is surely the most extraordinary position that ever occurred in a world championship match. Not so far as

93

Steinitz is concerned, for he later indicated that Black's game would be quite satisfactory after 16...♘g8. Truly a fantastic notion!

16...♘g4 17.♘h4! ♘e6 18.♗×g4 ♘×g5 19.♘f5!

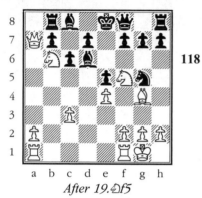

After 19.♘f5

White is steadily improving his position, while Black's game is pitifully disorganized.

19...♘e6

If Black tries 19...♘×e4, White wins by 20.♖fd1 ♗c7 21.♘×c8 ♖×c8 22.♕×b7 ♔d8 23.♕×c6 etc.

20.♖fd1! ♗c7 21.♘a8!

White's hard-hitting play is getting results; if now 21...♔d8 22.♘×c7 ♔×c7 23.♘d6 followed by ♖ab1 with an overwhelming position for White.

21...♖×a8 22.♕×a8 ♔d8

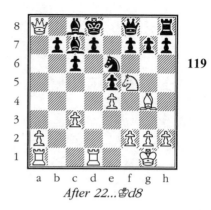

119

After 22...♔d8

White is now ready for decisive action: his pieces are admirably posted for attack, while Black's king is seriously exposed, his development in arrears, his queen out of play.

These are the situations, as we have seen earlier, where the attacker is justified in making heavy sacrifices of material. This explains White's next move.

23.♖×d7+! ♔×d7 24.♖d1+ Resigns

Even stubborn old Steinitz saw that it was time to give up the ghost.

Thus if 24...♗d6 25.♕b8! strengthens White's pin decisively.

Or 24...♘d4 25.c×d4 ♔e6 26.♘d6+! ♔×d6 27.♕a3+ c5 28.♕×c5#.

After 24...♘d4 25.c×d4 Black can try 25...e×d4, but after 26.♘×d4+ his helpless king must endure the concentrated fury of White's forces. That prospect is too grim for even a defensive genius like Steinitz.

So that's how Steinitz lost. But think back to your own play. Isn't it true you've lost many a game by being as stubborn and dogmatic as Steinitz? You've lost by playing the board and not the man. Instead, here's the way you should play:

How to Beat Your Equals

In the previous two games you've seen the right way to handle an opponent who's afflicted with technical or psychological weaknesses. When you're matched against a player who's your equal, you can still apply this system, but your play must be scrupulously sound. There's nothing in the advice I'm giving you here which means that you're to ignore "playing the board."

What it comes to is this: instead of *taking* chances, you *give* your opponent chances to go wrong. By confronting him with disagreeable alternatives, you sap his fighting spirit. Emanuel Lasker was a past master of this technique, and the following example shows his gamesmanship at its best.

Chigorin – Lasker
Evans Gambit
St. Petersburg 1895

1.e4 e5 2.♘f3 ♘c6 3.♗c4 ♗c5 4.b4 ♗×b4

Chigorin was a much greater master than Gunsberg (the victor in the previous game), and the Evans was his specialty. But Lasker confidently accepts the gambit, as he has no intention of handicapping himself a la Steinitz.

5.c3 ♗c5 6.0-0 d6!

Good, sound chess, and a vast improvement on Steinitz's weird 6...♕f6?.

7.d4

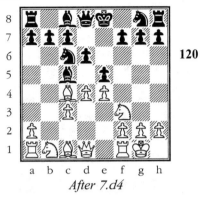

After 7.d4

7...♗b6!

Instead of giving White a powerful pawn center by 7...e×d4 8.c×d4 etc., Lasker actually offers his extra pawn back.

There's method in his madness. If White regains the pawn by 8.d×e5 d×e5 9.♕×d8+ ♘×d8 10.♘×e5, all his dreams of a glamorous attack are over. The drab ending would be dust and ashes to a spirited, aggressive player like Chigorin. On the other hand, Lasker, who played all types of positions with equal zest, would be in his element. No doubt about it – Chigorin shudders at the distasteful possibility of this ending.

So we have a superb example of Lasker's uncanny skill in playing the man. If Chigorin refrains from winning back the pawn, however, then Black always keeps a strong pawn in the center.

8.a4 ♘f6 9.♗b5 a6! 10.♗×c6+ b×c6 11.a5 ♗a7 12.d×e5 ♘×e4

95

Here too White can have his pawn back: 13.♕a4 ♘c5 14.♕xc6+ ♗d7 15.♕d5 0-0. But White's position would not be inviting.

13.♕e2 d5!

Lasker's central pawn position is sturdier than ever, and he has a magnificently centralized knight. But, more than that, he has stripped Chigorin of every trace of attacking possibilities. That's playing the man.

14.♘d4?! ♘xc3! 15.♘xc3 ♗xd4 16.♕d3 c5! 17.♕g3

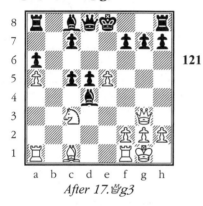

After 17.♕g3

Just for a moment it seems as if Chigorin is getting somewhere. If 17...0-0? 18.♗h6 ♗xe5 19.♕xe5 gxh6 20.♘xd5. Or 17...g6 18.♗g5 followed by ♗f6.

In either case, White has some attacking possibilities. But not the way Lasker plays it:

17...♗e6!

White's threat is no threat at all, for after 18.♕xg7? ♔d7 Black has a devastating attack along the open g-file.

Lasker has been playing good, sound chess, but, more than that, he has simply ignored White's threat. What could be more disparaging, more crushing? That's what I mean by playing the man.

18.♗g5 ♕d7 19.♖ac1 f6! 20.exf6 gxf6 21.♗f4 ♖g8

So Lasker has his open file just the same.

22.♕f3 0-0-0 23.♖fe1 c4!

Guards against the threatened 24.♕e2.

24.♕e2 ♗f5 25.♕a2?

White was lost in any event, but this hastens his downfall.

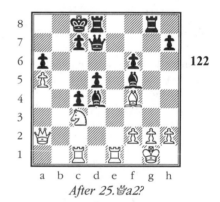

After 25.♕a2?

Black has local superiority on the kingside; his pieces are active.

White lacks defensive resources, and his queen is out of play.

In short, a brilliant sacrifice in indicated.

25...♖xg2+! 26.♔h1

For if 26.♔xg2 ♗h3+ 27.♔h1 ♕g4 and mate follows.

26...♖×f2 Resigns

If 27.♘e2 ♗e4+ wins. Or 27.♗d2 ♕d6 etc.

This remarkably clear-cut and enlightening game convincingly points up the moral: play the man, not the board. True, Lasker played the board as well, for he was a sound and vigorous tactician. But over and above his technical skill was his ability to confront his opponent with a shattering choice that robbed Chigorin of all further taste for the game. Lasker's magnificent seventh move proves that beyond the peradventure of a doubt. For Lasker knew darned well that Chigorin, trapped in a cleft stick, would never accept the pawn at the cost of losing whatever attack was left. Thus he forced Chigorin to play on without conviction, without hope – and at the cost of giving Lasker a powerful center pawn (see Chapter 3).

There you have a valuable lesson for your own games. You don't play the man. You don't exploit your opponent's weaknesses. You don't confront him with fateful choices which force him to lose his taste for the game of forfeit his positional advantage.

By failing to do these things, you make it easy for your opponent. You make it hard for yourself. And that's why you lose at chess.

Chapter 8

You Lose Because You're Easily Bored

Positions that look routine, appear even, and seem colorless have a bad effect on your play. They tend to bore you, make you lose interest, cause you to grow careless.

Take the following position, for example:

Janowsky – Berger
Carlsbad 1907

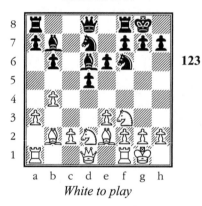

123

White to play

If you had White in this position, you'd find it hard to work up any interest. White is in no great danger, but on the other hand he doesn't seem to have any particularly inviting goal before him. In short, a typically dull and uninspiring position.

Be that as it may, my contention is this: faced with such a situation, you tend to become bored; you lose interest; you grow careless; and in due course you lose.

What can you do to overcome your aversion to these colorless positions? First, you must learn to distinguish between positions that are really barren of possibilities and those which only *seem* colorless. The great masters, for example, have the knack of uncovering possibilities that remain forever hidden from the rest of us.

Alekhine had this knack to an amazing degree. Euwe called him "a poet who creates a work of art out of something that would hardly inspire another man to send home a picture post card."

Spielmann, himself a great attacking player, said plaintively: "I can comprehend Alekhine's combinations well enough; but where he gets his attacking chances from and how he infuses such life into the very opening – that is beyond me."

Well, then, what do we do about the positions that are *really* colorless? Remember, these make up the majority of positions in chess, just as they make up the majority of situations in real life. It would be very pleasant if every game gave us scope for a slashing attack or imaginative combinations. But in actual fact the number of such games is very, very limited.

What advice, then, can I offer you about these positions that *seem* totally devoid of interest? What clue can guide you?

This is a difficult subject – so difficult, in fact, that no chess writer I know of has ever tried to tackle it. In thinking about it, I had to start from scratch. My thoughts went somewhat along these lines:

Suppose we take a master game that starts off colorlessly and then winds up with a decisive result. There's a certain point at which we can say the game is still even, and there's a certain point later on where it's become clear that someone is going to win. And, just to clarify the problem, let's assume that victory is not the result of a crass blunder by the opponent.

So far we've narrowed down the explanation of victory to a fairly small zone. What has happened in this short span of moves? One side has given way. But how? And why?

The Winning Technique

There are two reasons why a player is able to build up a win in a colorless position. Basically, the secret is to offer the opponent alternatives. One of these alternatives may leave his position intact, the other may weaken him slightly.

If you opponent selects the right course, the position remains level. But if he chooses the other, his position begins to deteriorate imperceptibly. Mind you, he's not yet lost. He begins to wonder. He becomes unsure of himself.

The next time he's offered an alternative he's more likely to go wrong. The process is repeated, and eventually he finds – much too late –

that the game has drifted out of his control. He has a lost game.

There's another reason for drifting into a lost game without making any overt blunder. The very colorlessness of the situation breeds carelessness. Chess doesn't allow for continual flouting of the right move. A few sins of omission, and a fairly easygoing and characterless situation is transformed into one that bristles with lasting difficulties.

Missing the Point

Now let's see how the colorless position in Diagram 123 was arrived at and how the subsequent play proceeded. The position came about from routine and innocuous moves. Precisely because these moves were so matter of fact and lacking in tension, Black mistakenly thought he could just coast along. White, on the other hand, was well aware of the treacherous nature of the opening play and therefore watched alertly for his opportunity to exploit the flaws in Black's policy. White's superior insight eventually pays off in the form of a winning position.

Janowsky – Berger
Queen's Pawn Opening
Carlsbad 1907

1.d4 d5 2.♘f3 c5 3.d×c5 e6 4.e3 ♗×c5

A position that looks quite colorless. Both players have blocked the queen bishop by advancing the e-pawn one square.

5.♗e2

A lack-luster substitute for the more aggressive 5.♗d3.

99

5...♘f6 6.0-0 0-0 7.a3 b6 8.b4 ♗d6 9.♗b2 ♗b7 10.♘bd2 ♘bd7

And so, as both players are completing their development sedately, we arrive at the position of Diagram 123. Tactical possibilities are nil. And yet this game was destined to win a brilliancy prize!

11.c4 ♛e7

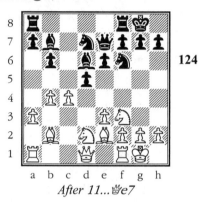

124

After 11...♛e7

Black (who will eventually lose this game) certainly has nothing to fear at this point. He's actually ahead in development, and his dark-square bishop is more aggressively placed than his White opposite number.

But… just a minute. Here's the first tiny cloud no bigger than a man's hand. Is the black dark-square bishop aggressively placed? Yes, if there is a possibility of kingside attack. However, there is no such possibility: the position is too even.

But if there's no possibility of kingside attack, then the emphasis will be on play in the center and on the queenside. In that case, the modestly posted white light-square bishop may be more advantageously placed. Can it be that crafty Janowsky was well aware of that? Let's see:

12.c×d5

Giving Black his first choice of alternatives. If now 12...e×d5 Black has a strong hold on the center, with ...♘e4 to follow. But his d-pawn would be isolated – a lasting weakness – and his light-square bishop would have no scope. Therefore:

12...♗×d5

The right recapture. Black gives the bishop a long diagonal. But now Janowsky creates another alternative:

13.♘d4!

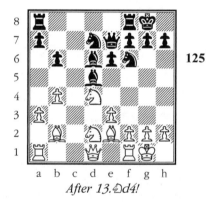

125

After 13.♘d4!

Now a great light dawns.

The c6-square is a "hole" – it isn't commanded by pawns and never can be. Hence, if White succeeds in removing Black's protective light-square bishop, he may be able to occupy this hole by ♘c6. In that case, White would get a commanding position. (You'll see why later on.)

Suddenly we find that the colorless position is not quite so colorless. The game now has an Ariadne thread, as in the classic Greek myth which tells how

Ariadne laid down a thread on the floors of the Labyrinth to guide the hero Theseus through the innumerable rooms of the maze. Once we have such a guiding idea, the game becomes somewhat easier.

And yet – there are still dangers. Black has three ways to react. He may underestimate the threat; he may be thrown into a panic by it; he may meet it alertly, yet without committing himself.

White's plan, roughly, is to play ♗f3, getting rid of Black's guardian bishop. Then he can continue with b4-b5 and wait for a favorable opportunity to further his plan. Black's indicated reply is 13...♖ac8, giving more protection to the c6-square and placing his rook on a useful open file. That would be alert yet noncommittal procedure.

13...a5

But this is something else again. Black provokes b4-b5 in order to centralize his queen knight with ...♘c5. A laudable aim, to be sure, but he's helping White to carry out his plan!

14.b5 ♘c5

Black isn't lost. He isn't even in danger. But it's true he's courting danger. The position still looks colorless, but under the surface some sinister possibilities are taking shape.

15.♗f3

According to plan.

However, Black can parry that plan easily by playing 15...♘fe4!, gaining further centralization and an excellent position.

15...♘d3?

But Black chooses the wrong alternative! Yet the move is so insidiously plausible. The Janowsky bishops were always dreaded weapons, hence Burger's eagerness to get rid of White's remaining bishop. In his haste, Black forgets that he is parting with the knight that he has just anchored so powerfully at c5.

16.♗×d5 ♘×b2 17.♕b3 ♘×d5 18.♕×b2

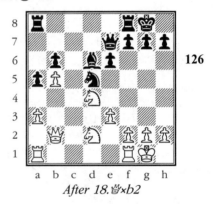

126

After 18.♕×b2

Now White is all set to play ♘c6, preventing ...♖d8 and gradually achieving a strangle hold on the open d-file.

Black can prevent this, at least for a while, but each preventive move is made at the cost of giving ground in some other respect.

18...♕f6

Pinning the knight and thus preventing ♘c6.

19.♖ac1

The plausible 19.♘e4? would not do because of 19...♗×h2+ 20.♔×h2 ♕h4+ etc.

19...罝ac8 20.豐b3

Renewing the threat of ♘c6.

20...豐h6?

This deplorably superficial move threatens mate, but at what a cost! Black's queen is now out of bounds on the kingside, unable to lend a helping hand in the struggle on the queenside.

Here we're reminded of an important feature of Chapter 5, but with a reverse twist. There we noted that when an attack is started on the kingside, it is likely to succeed if the defender's queen is out of play.

But in the situation of Diagram 127 we find the reverse holds good. The main theater of action at this point is the queenside, and Black is fatally handicapped by the absence of his queen from that threatened sector. And why? Because he plays footsie with a one-move mating threat.

21.g3

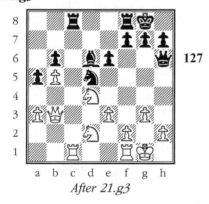

After 21.g3

Black has a positionally lost game. If now 21...♘e7 22.♘e4 ♗b8 23.♘c6 ♘xc6 24.bxc6 ♗c7 25.罝fd1 罝fd8 26.罝d7! and White's powerful passed pawn must win the game for him.

This variation has two significant features. One is that White has had his way in concentrating the play on the center and queenside. The other feature, as we've seen, is that Black's queen is badly placed, being on the wrong side of the board.

21...♗c5

A trap which shouldn't work. The idea is that if now 22.♘c6! Black replies 22...♘xe3?! 23.fxe3 ♗xe3+ 24.♔g2 ♗xd2. But Black overlooks that in that case 25.♘e7+ is crushing.

22.♘2f3

And White overlooks this possibility too.

Now Black has good chances to hold the position with 22...♘e7!.

22...豐h5

Preventing ♘c6 because of the attack on White's other knight.

23.♔g2

Even now Black can hold the position if he plays with due alertness.

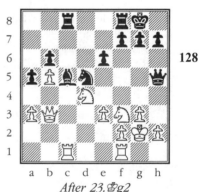

After 23.♔g2

Now Black can still hold the game with 23...♘e7!.

23...♘f6? 24.♘c6!

At last! Watch Black's game crumble.

24...♔h8 25.♖fd1! h6 26.♖c4!

Now, after the preliminary groping stage, the game suddenly takes on a furious tempo. Black's misplaced queen now becomes the target – and Black's king too. All because Black is immobilized for counterplay.

26...♘d5 27.♖h4! ♕g6

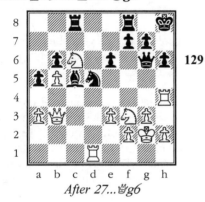

After 27...♕g6

28.♘ce5

The knight heads for even greener pastures, driving Black's queen to a miserable spot. (If now 28...♕f6? 29.♘d7 wins the exchange.)

28...♕h7 29.e4! ♘e7 30.♖d7! ♖ce8 31.♘g5! ♕g8 32.♕c3!!

What magnificent progress White has made after his colorless opening, thanks to Black's inexact play! White threatens 33.♖×h6+! g×h6 34.♘g6# or 34.♘e×f7#.

32...f6 33.♖×e7! Resigns

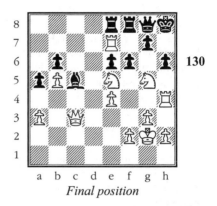

Final position

Although three white pieces are *en prise*, Black is helpless.

If the rook is captured, then 34.♘g6#.

If 33...f×g5 34.♖×h6+! g×h6 35.♘g6#.

If 33...f×e5 34.♖×h6+! g×h6 35.♕×e5+ leads to mate.

This is an uncommonly instructive game. At move 15 Black had a playable game. At move 18 – *without having made any obvious blunder* – he had a lost position! It was his 15th move that compromised his position. His misfortune was that 15...♘d3? was both plausible and uninspired.

But there's more to it than that. Black's 13...a5, though not a blunder, was psychologically wrong, because it committed him too far. It laid the psychological basis for a later mistake. It is these innocent-looking moves that you must guard against.

Give a man enough rope...

Emanuel Lasker was a past master in the handling of seemingly colorless positions. He was content to go along placidly, confident that his opponent would entangle himself sooner than he would – either through carelessness of befuddlement. Again and again Lasker made the experienced masters look like helpless children. Consider the following example:

Lasker – Tarrasch
Ruy Lopez
Nuremberg 1896

1.e4 e5 2.♘f3 ♘c6 3.♗b5 a6 4.♗×c6

A colorless move par excellence. If anything, Black might be considered to have the better of it, as he's left with two bishops against a bishop and knight.

4...d×c6

If now 5.♘×e5 Black recovers the pawn by 5...♕g5 or 5...♕d4.

5.♘c3

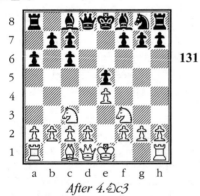

131

After 4.♘c3

Now Black has an effective continuation in 5...f6 (protecting his e-pawn). Then after 6.d3 ♗d6 7.♗e3 ♘e7 8.♕d2 c5 he has a safe, solid position with prospects for his bishops

after the position opens up later on.

But Black's wide choice of moves proves too much for him.

5...♗c5

A plausible developing move. On 6.♘×e5 he plans 6...♗×f2+ 7.♔×f2 ♕d4+ etc.

6.d3 ♗g4

Black's development has been high, wide, and handsome. Yet White's very next move raises questions.

7.♗e3!

Psychologically very troublesome for Black. If he swaps bishops, he gives White an open f-file.

If he retreats his dark-square bishop, he acknowledges that his sixth move was shortsighted. (Note how craftily Lasker undermines his opponent's self-confidence! Black's position is still eminently playable, but he's beginning to be nagged by doubts.)

7...♕d6

A compromise. He allows the swap, but goes on with his development. Even so, the position offers more problems than Black realizes.

8.♗×c5 ♕×c5

Still a rather colorless position.

9.♕d2!

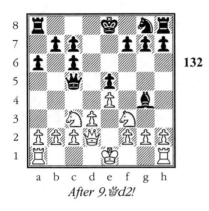

132

After 9.♕d2!

Lasker's last move is very clever. By *unpinning* his knight, he makes Black question the value of 6...♗g4. And by threatening to win a pawn by 10.♕g5, he reinforces that impression.

However, by playing 9...f6 Black would be perfectly safe. Instead, having lost his grip, he plays:

9...♗×f3 10.g×f3 ♘e7 11.0-0-0 ♘g6 12.♕e3!

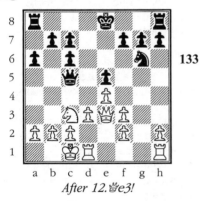

133

After 12.♕e3!

The crisis. Black is reluctant to castle on the kingside in the face of the open g-file he has created for White. Black must therefore think in terms of castling on the queenside. Since Black plans to castle on the queenside, Lasker's last move creates a serious dilemma for

him. If he avoids the exchange of queens by 12...♕d6, for example, this is what might happen: 13.a3 0-0-0 14.♕a7! (threatening 15.♕a8+ and 16.♕×b7). So Tarrasch decides to get rid of the queens.

12...♕×e3+ 13.f×e3

Now White has strengthened his central pawn position, creating a later possibility of f3-f4, which would further cramp Black's game.

But even now Black is by no means lost, and in the eyes of average players nothing very interesting or important has happened. Yet Black is already demoralized, having been subtly persuaded that his judgment is poor.

13...♖d8 14.♘e2

Getting ready for f3-f4, which will constrict Black's game. But Lasker characteristically lets this threat hang over Black's head, in that way increasing the psychological menace.

14...f6 15.♖hg1 ♔f7?

The first definite step toward perdition. It would have been safer to castle – for reasons that will soon become clear.

16.♖df1

Another menacing move. Note how Lasker maneuvers on the files opened for him by Black.

16...♖he8 17.♘g3! ♘f8

In order to keep out White's knight by ...g6.

18.f4

With a view to 19.fxe5 ♖xe5 20.d4 ♖ee8 21.e5 and White has powerful pressure.

18...c5 19.♘h5!

Black is lost!

If 19...♘g6 20.f5 followed by 21.♖xg7+ and wins. Or 19...♘e6 20.f5 winning, as 20...♘g5 is refuted by 21.h4.

19...g6

Apparently the only chance. But White has a stinging refutation.

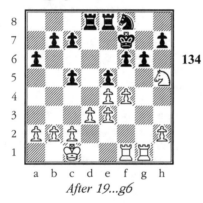

After 19...g6

20.fxe5!

Remember what was said in an earlier chapter about tactical finesses that win endgames?

Suddenly Black realizes that if 20...gxh5? White can play 21.♖xf6+ ♔e7 22.♖g7#!

20...♖xe5 21.♘xf6

With a pawn to the good and a vastly superior position, Lasker had no trouble winning the ending. Play it out yourself and see.

Here are the concluding moves:

21...♔g7 22.♖f2 h5 23.♘d5 c6 24.♘f4 c4 25.♖fg2 ♖d6 26.h4 cxd3 27.cxd3 ♔f7 28.♖g5 ♖xg5 29.♖xg5 ♖f6 30.e5 ♖f5 31.♖xf5+ gxf5 32.d4 ♔e7 33.♔d2 c5 34.♔d3 cxd4 35.exd4 ♔d8 36.d5 ♔d7 37.♔d4 ♔c7 38.b4 ♔d7 39.♔c5 ♔c7 40.d6+ ♔d7 41.♔d5 Resigns

From these two seemingly colorless games you can learn a great deal.

Having the impression, as you have, that the possibilities are limited in colorless positions, you become easily bored. Then, as you've seen, it takes only a careless more or two to place you in a hopeless predicament. You can therefore draw the following conclusions:

If you underestimate the possibilities in colorless positions, you lose because you soon find yourself faced with formidable threats, largely because you're asleep at the switch.

If you see threats where none really exist, you lose because you compromise your position by your excessive anxiety.

If you fail to play alertly, if you become bored and careless, you lose because the balance of power slips away from you. The equilibrium of the position is disturbed, and by no means to your advantage.

You can't have Nesselrode pie with every meal, and you can't have brilliant, colorful positions in every game. You have to learn to live with these routine positions and accept them for what they are. If you get bored easily, or if you lose patience quickly, you'll not only lose at chess, you'll continue to lose.

Chapter 9

You Lose Because You're Lazy

You dislike difficult situations and you shun complications. Why? Because you're too lazy to buckle down and solve the problems that arise in the course of a game.

And so you lose – and you deserve to lose, because you're inconsistent. You get into a bad position because you hate to exchange queens. Yet, when you find yourself in a situation that seems complicated precisely because the queens are still on the board, you dodge the issue.

"What's this?" you answer. "Am I supposed to work at my hobby?" Certainly. Why not?

If you were a stamp collector, you'd be busy with watermarks and perforations and errors and microscopically different varieties.

If you played golf you'd spend every spare minute on the course polishing your shots; you'd pay good money to a pro for expert advice; you'd read every new book on the game with avid interest. So why be lackadaisical about your chess?

And remember this: let it be known that you dislike complications and, believe me, your opponents will feed you a steady diet of complications. By dodging the issue, you'll only create new troubles for yourself.

In chess there are often crucial positions in which you must meet the issue squarely. At such times the hard way is the only way to win, while the easy way is... the easy way to lose.

Winning the Hard Way

Sammy Reshevsky is famous for his grit and determination. When a position looks ripe for resigning, he digs in, sets up his defenses, and makes it so hard for his opponent that he eventually escapes with a draw – or even a win. Here is one of his outstanding efforts. It shows what tenacious defense can achieve:

Ulvestad – Reshevsky
U.S. Open Championship 1939

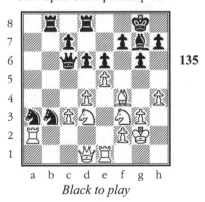

135

Black to play

Both of Black's unfortunate knights are under attack. The knight at b3 is defended, the other one needs to be guarded.

Note that retreat is impossible, for 1...♘b5? allows 2.♕×b3. Or if 1...♘c4 2.♘b4, and White wins the exchange as Black has nothing better than 2...♖×b4, etc. Nor does 1...♖a8? work, as 2.♕×b3 again becomes possible.

Reshevsky grimly finds the only way, despite the fact that he has to make 13 moves in less than a minute.

1...♕a8!

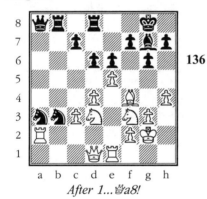

After 1...♕a8!

Imagine walking into such an uncomfortable pin!

Yet Black can hold the position even after 2.♗c1, when there follows 2...♘×c1 3.♕×c1 ♖b3 4.♕a1 (or 4.♘b4 c5! 5.♘c2 ♖×c3 6.♖e3 ♖×c2!, and Black wins. These are indeed remarkable variations!) 4...♖db8 5.♘c1 ♖b1!.

Nor does Black have to fear 2.e×d6 c×d6 3.♘c1 e5! 4.♗e3 e×d4 with two possibilities:
(a) 5.c×d4 ♕a4 6.♔g1 ♖b4 and Black is holding his own.
(b) 5.♗×d4 ♗×d4 6.c×d4 ♘×c1 7.♕×c1 ♖b3 8.♖e3 ♖×e3 9.♕×e3 ♘c4!. Here the big point is that if 10.♖×a8? ♘×e3+ and Black wins.

Trust Reshevsky to find these diabolical finesses in a split second!

2.♘b4 ♘×d4!

Beautiful play, taking advantage of the pin by Black's queen on the long diagonal, and the masked action of his rook on the d-file.

3.c×d4

Or 3.♕×d4 d×e5 and Black recovers the piece advantageously.

3...♖×b4 4.♕d3 ♖a4

Reshevsky is prepared for 5.e×d6 c×d6 6.♖ea1 – for then comes 6...♗×d4!! and if 7.♖×a3 ♗×a1 wins for Black.

5.♖ea1

Now it seems that Black has played his last trick.

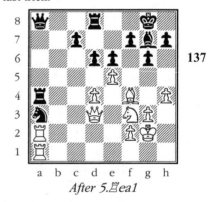

After 5.♖ea1

In a flash Reshevsky finds the only move:

5...d×e5! 6.♖×a3

If now 6.♗×e5 ♗×e5 7.♖×a3 ♖×a3 8.♖×a3 ♕d5 and Black's bishop is safe!

6...♖×a3 7.♖×a3 ♕d5!

Now everything becomes clear. If 8.♗xe5 ♗xe5 and Black has regained the piece. If 8.♗e3 (or some other bishop retreat), then 8...e4 still regains the piece!

8.♕c3 exf4 9.♕xc7 fxg3

And Reshevsky won easily in another few moves, on the basis of his material advantage.

This is my favorite example of what a determined player can achieve in the face of desperate odds.

Meet the Challenge!

But few players have the great fighting ability of a Reshevsky. Most players, in fact, have a bad habit of adopting mechanical defenses which they *know* are inadequate. Perhaps they're fatalistic; perhaps they're listless. But could anything be more foolish than this attitude which caves in without a battle?

When the situation is desperate beyond recall, that's the time to seek a saving line that seems utterly fantastic. After all, if the situation is really bad, what do you have to lose?

To see the problem in its most glaring form, let's look at a position in which one player finds a magnificent resource and his opponent throws away the game with a lack-luster reply:

Morphy – Lichtenhein
U.S. Championship 1857

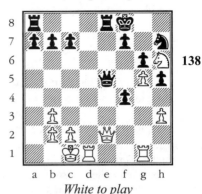

138

White to play

Morphy has given up two pawns for an unsound attack, and he's about to lose a third pawn. In fact, after White loses his g-pawn he will lose his knight as well.

In the seemingly hopeless situation Morphy plays a move of pure genius:

1.♖d7!!?

Truly beautiful play.

If now 1...♕xe2 2.♖xf7#.

And if 1...♖e7 2.♕xe5 ♖xe5 3.♖xf7+ ♔e8 4.♖xh7 and wins. (The position of Black's knight seems a misfortune that cannot be remedied.)

Finally, Black sees that if 1...♘xg5 2.♖xg5! is the reply.

What is Black to do? Morphy's brilliant stroke has confused him badly. He tries a half-hearted defense, which is refuted in a few moves:

1...♕g7? 2.♕c4!

109

Renewing the mate threat, so that after 2...♘xg5 3.♖xg5 Black cannot capture the knight.

2...♖e7 3.♖xe7 ♔xe7 4.♖e1+ Resigns

For if 4...♔f8 5.♕c5#. And if 4...♔d7 5.♕d5+ forces mate next move.

What is appalling about Black's defeat is the utter stupidity with which he marched to sure disaster. How could a player of Lichtenhein's strength walk right into checkmate? But that's just what he did – and so do many others.

Instead of this nightmare finish, Black had a satisfactory defense! The moves that make up that defense are very clever, and yet there were two reasons why those moves should not have been too hard to find.

The first reason is that the way Black actually played was pointless. He had to lose with those moves, therefore he should have looked for something else. To a player who is determined and energetic such a situation is stimulating rather than depressing.

The second reason why Black should have found the right defense is that each of the moves that make it up are counterattacking. To me, the very essence of chess is counterattack. Don't you agree? At any rate, let's have another look at the position after 1.♖d7!!? to see how Black should have played:

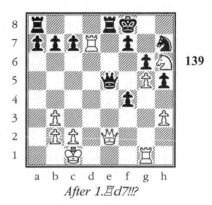

139

After 1.♖d7!!?

The right move for Black was:

1...♘xg5!!

If you'll turn back to page 109, you'll note that I dismissed this move with the brief comment that it was to be answered by 2.♖xg5!. Perhaps, like Lichtenhein, you were dazzled by that brilliant reply. If so – again, like Lichtenhein – you gave up hope too quickly.

2. ♖xg5!

Brilliant, to be sure, but don't forget that a brilliant move is not necessarily conclusive.

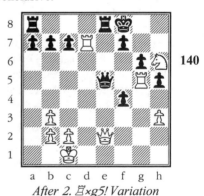

140

After 2. ♖xg5! Variation

But White still threatens mate and still leaves his queen *en prise*. For in the event of 2...♛×e2? or 2...♛×g5? he has 3.♖×f7#.

2...♛f6!!

Bravo! To be brilliant is commendable; but to be cold-blooded in the face of your opponent's brilliancy is even more commendable!

Black's last move accomplishes a great deal:

It defends the threatened mate.

It unleashes a valid threat against White's queen.

It keeps White's king rook under attack.

And, incidentally, it sets a neat trap, to wit:

If White, in an exalted mood of brilliant inspiration, plays 3.♛×h5?! hoping for 3...g×h5?? 4.♖g8#, Black smashes the attack once and for all by playing 3...♖ad8!!.

If then 4.♛g4 ♖×d7 5.♛×d7 and Black still cannot capture the tantalizing rook. But he can play 5...f3! and this wins: 6.♖g1 f2 7.♖f1 ♖e1+, etc.

This delightful variation has a moral: Black wins by counterattack.

3.♛c4

The only move, but apparently very powerful, as it threatens mate in two.

3...♖e1+ 4.♔d2 ♖e7 5.♖×e7 ♛×e7

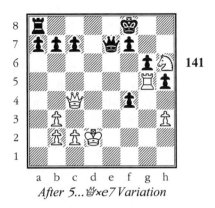

After 5...♛×e7 Variation

Now Black threatens 6...♛e3+ 7.♔d1 ♖d8+ 8.♖d5 ♛f3+! with an easy win.

Now we see what a totally different kind of position arises when Black fights back.

White has a piece for three pawns, but his position bristles with difficulties. Thus, if he plays 6.♖e5 Black interpolates 6...♖d8+!. Now White's king cannot cross to the e-file, so that after 7.♔c1 ♛f6, Black has the potent threat of ...f3 followed by ...f2 and ...f1♛+. (And for good measure Black threatens ...♔g7, picking up the knight.)

Suppose that White tries a different tack in the position of Diagram 141: 6.♛×f4 ♖d8+ 7.♔c3 ♛e1+ 8.♔c4 ♛e2+. Now if White knows what's good for him, he'll take a perpetual check with 9.♔c3 9...♛e1+ etc. For 9.♔c5 ♛×c2+ 10.♔b4 ♛d2+ 11.♔×d2 ♖×d2 when Black again threatens ...♔g7, winning the knight and thus remaining with a won endgame.

We've looked at a great many moves and a great many variations since Diagram 138. Let's boil them down to a single, straightforward conclusion:

If Black had defended himself with real determination (beginning with

1...♘xg5!!), he would have had at least a draw, and perhaps a win.

Now you may say this whole suggested line of play is too difficult to see. Granted, it's difficult – especially for the lazy player. But that's just the point: the line that's easy to find, the line that Black actually played, loses out of hand. Hence the difficult line – *the one that makes trouble for White* – is the only one that deserves consideration.

Let's get this straight: you don't have to see ahead to the very last move. All I ask of you is to choose the defense that allows you to fight, to hold out, to create obstacles for your opponent. The easy way, the fatalistic way – these will get you nowhere.

If you fight back as hard as you can, you *may* still lose. But on the other hand you have at least a *chance* to draw or even win. But if you take the lazy course, you're *sure to lose*.

In contrast to Black's spineless collapse in the previous example is White's beautifully resourceful counterattack in the following position:

Rossolimo – Amateur
Paris 1944

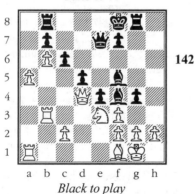

142

Black to play

Instead of playing 1...♗xe3 and 2...gxf3, Black tries what looks like a decisive attack along the open h-file:

1...♗xh2+?! 2.♔xh2 ♕h4+ 3.♔g1 ♖h8

Black threatens checkmate. It seems that White has nothing better than 4.♕xh8+ ♕xh8 when he is unable to play 5.♘xf5 because of 5...♕xa1.

Apparently, then, White is condemned to give up his queen because of the threatened checkmate. However, he finds a magnificent counterattack.

You may ask: how does one find these ingenious resources? The answer is that necessity is truly the mother of invention. The position is desperate. You know that you must find a good move or else you're sunk. Your sharp awareness of the brutal crisis should spur you on. Don't give way to despair!

143

After 3...♖a8

4.♕g7+!!

If now 4...♔xg7 5.♘xf5+ followed by 6.♘xh4 and White wins easily with his extra piece.

4...♔e8 5.♕e5+!

This rules out 5...♔f8 because of the reply 6.♕xb8+ followed by 7.♘xf5+ winning Black's queen. And if 5...♔d8 6.♕c7+! forces the same variation.

5...♔d7

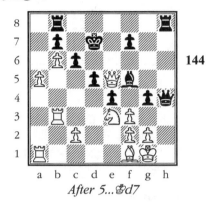

After 5...♔d7

Black hopes for 6.♕xf5+? ♔d8!! and wins!

6.♕d6+!! Resigns

Again, if 6...♔xd6 7.♘xf5+ and 8.♘xh4 winning easily. If 6...♔c8 7.♕c7#. And if 6...♔e8 7.♕xb8+ wins.

White's brilliant play is an impressive example of the power of centralized pieces.

You lose because you dawdle

Lucky indeed is the player who can face a crisis as perceptively and incisively as Rossolimo.

Your own attitude is different. When you see a troublesome situation, you brush it under the carpet. You hope that by ignoring it, you can somehow make it disappear. Instead, of course, it only gets worse.

And it gets worse in a number of ways. You give your opponent all the time in the world to build up his position comfortably, getting his forces into the most favorable setup for the kill. You give him nothing to worry about, nothing to hold back his cumulative gathering of force. Meanwhile, you naturally grow more helpless as your position gets worse.

You lose, in short, because you see disaster looming but you do nothing to try to hold it back. You owe it to yourself at least to make some effort to fight back. You may discover, to your astonishment, that the inevitable may not be inevitable after all!

I firmly believe it's possible to make a good recovery after mismanaging the earlier part of the game. If you're skeptical, that's perfectly understandable. So, let me show you a game that proved a turning point in my own playing career. In the opening and early middlegame my play was so feckless that I realized I deserved to lose. I was in despair. I knew that if Capablanca or Alekhine or one of the other great ones had the black pieces, he'd make mincemeat of my position.

Like many youngsters, I was very dogmatic. I'd botched the game, I deserved to lose, and that was that. But in this game I learned what it takes to make a mature chess player. Fully and honestly aware of how badly I had played, I was nevertheless ashamed of myself for despairing so readily.

After all, my opponent was *not* Capablanca or Alekhine. Why not make victory as tough as possible for him?

Maybe he'd become overconfident. Maybe he'd blunder. Maybe – who knows? – he'd overstep the time limit. Such things have happened!

So, instead of waiting fatalistically for disaster, I fought back as best I could. I knew that I had a lost game. Yet, rather than drift ingloriously toward certain defeat, I preferred to give my opponent as hard a time as possible.

You can do the same in your own games. Remember, the lazy way is the sure way to lose. And the "hard" way is not so hard when you realize that it brings results – good results.

I've chosen a game of my own, not by way of showing off, but for a totally different reason. My play in the early part of the game was very bad – no duffer could do worse. Because of that, I had to sweat through the rest of the game. What I learned was so valuable that I want to tell you what went on and what I learned from it. In that way, you can learn from my bad moves and perhaps avoid similar difficulties in your own games.

Reinfeld – Dornbach
Queen's Gambit Declined
Metropolitan Chess League 1926

1.d4 d5 2.c4 e6 3.♘c3 ♘f6 4.♘f3 ♘bd7 5.♗g5 c6 6.c×d5

To avoid the Cambridge Springs Defense (6.e3 ♕a5 etc.).

6...e×d5 7.e3 ♗e7

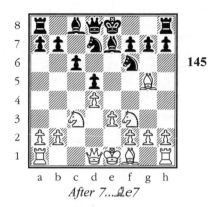

145

After 7...♗e7

Black is poised to free himself with ...♘e4. White should prevent this with 8.♕c2! (if then 8...♘e4? 9.♘×e4 d×e4 10.♕×e4, winning a pawn).

8.♗d3 ♘e4!

If now 9.♘×e4? d×e4 wins a piece for Black!

9.♗×e7 ♕×e7 10.0-0 0-0 11.♖c1 f5

Black has equalized – to say the least. White's opening strategy is completely discredited. Upset by that realization, he lets his position deteriorate.

12.♕b3? ♘df6 13.♗×e4? f×e4 14.♘e5 ♔h8 15.♘a4? ♘g4 16.♘×g4 ♗×g4 17.♖c2? ♖f7

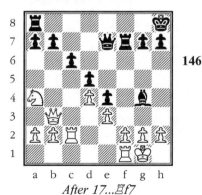

146

After 17...♖f7

It would be hard to find a worse example of opening play than White has shown in this game. He's generously helped Black to set up a strong attacking position, and at the same time he's systematically removed his own pieces from the threatened kingside.

White realizes that if he waits passively for the coming storm, he'll be helpless against such possibilities as ...♕g5 followed by ...♗h3 or ...♗f3; or else ...♖-f6-h6 followed by ...♕h4. He sees that he can't improve his position, while Black can strengthen his game in a number of ways.

Consequently White decides to force the issue, provoking an immediate attack before the position gets any worse. Mind you, he'll still have a difficult game, but at least he'll be able to make a fight of it.

18.h3!?

Not an easy decision, as White knew his king would be hounded to the c3-square in the coming attack!

18...♗×h3!

After 18...♗h5 Black's attacking formation is not so effective, and White may be able to consolidate with ♘c3-e2-g3.

19.g×h3 ♖f3

With many threats against White's exposed king. The chief one, perhaps, is ...♕h4 followed by ...♖×h3.

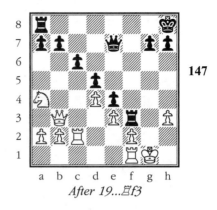

After 19...♖f3

White's king must run away.

20.♖fc1! ♕d7 21.♔f1! ♕×h3+ 22.♔e2 b5 23.♘c5 a5

If instead 23...♖×f2+? 24.♔×f2 ♖f8+ 25.♔g1! and White is safe.

24.♖f1 ♕g4 25.♔e1 h5

Black has two pawns for his piece, and his pressure still continues.

26.♖c1 ♖af8 27.♕d1 ♖×f2!

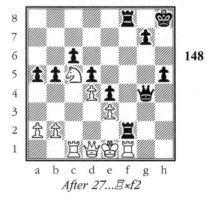

After 27...♖×f2

Now Black has picked up a third pawn for his piece, and his attack rolls on.

White dare not play 28.♕×g4 because of 28...♖×f1+! 29.♔d2 (not 29.♔e2?? ♖8f2#) 29...h×g4 when Black is the exchange and three pawns ahead.

115

28.♖×f2 ♕g1+ 29.♔d2

The only move.

29...♖×f2+ 30.♔c3

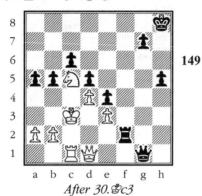

149

After 30.♔c3

Now Black should play 30...♕h2 when White plays 31.♖c2! (not 31.♕h1?? ♖c2+!! and wins) and it's still a fight.*

30...♕×d1 31.♖×d1 ♖e2 32.♖h1! b4+

If now 32...♖×e3+ 33.♔d2 followed by ♖×h5+. Or 32...g6 33.♖h3! ♔g7 34.♘b7 a4 35.♘d8!.

33.♔b3 ♖×e3+ 34.♔a4 g6

Black has four pawns for the piece, but he must lose, despite his three passed pawns.

The point is that White's king is no longer menaced and is now free to massacre the hostile pawns.

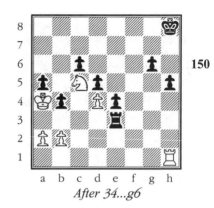

150

After 34...g6

35.♔×a5 ♖e2 36.♔b6!

Threatens 37.a4! b×a3 38.b×a3 followed by the advance of the pawn to the eighth ran. (Remember what we said about the importance of queening pawns in the endgame?)

36...♖×b2 37.♔×c6 ♖×a2 38.♔×d5

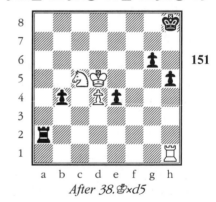

151

After 38.♔×d5

White has only one pawn left, but that pawn is a candidate for queening and there's nothing Black can do about it.

38...e3 39.♔e5

Making way for the advance of the d-pawn.

39...罝f2 40.罝e1 e2 41.♘e4 罝f8 42.罝xe2 ♔g7 43.d5 ♔h6 44.d6 h4 45.d7

The advance of this pawn is decisive.

45...g5 46.♘f6

Threatens 47.♘e8 and 48.d8♕.

46...罝d8 47.♔f5 b3 48.罝e7! Resigns

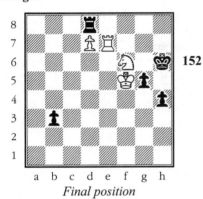

Final position

Black is helpless. If 48...罝h8 49.d8♕! 罝xd8 50.罝h7 #.

From this game you can see how you can often salvage a desperate position by meeting the crisis head-on.

On the other hand, if you dodge the issue, you lose – and lose without a fight. By closing your eyes to the dangers which threaten you, you play into your opponent's hands. By temporizing, by hesitating, you condemn yourself to a situation where you can no longer hold the game. By giving up hope too quickly, you actually create new dangers for yourself. By being too lazy to fight, you make it impossible to fight. And as long as you succumb to inertia and laziness you'll continue to lose at chess.

Chapter 10

You Lose Because You're Stubborn

You have prejudices and preconceived notions – and you refuse to give them up. Of all the faults in your play, this is the most inexcusable. For what good does it do to show you why you lost at chess if you're too set in you ways to change?

Chances are, though, that you're inflexible because you fail to realize that sticking to preconceived notions leads to defeat. Once you're shown the inevitable consequences of this attitude you may perhaps change your approach. That change, I grant you, is not an easy one; what's happened is that generalizations which were once serviceable have now hardened into harmful clichés. It requires a real effort of will if you're to cast them aside.

Why is it, for example, that you refuse a draw in any or all positions? Forcing a position beyond what it can legitimately yield is a dangerous policy and often leads to a loss which you could easily have avoided.

Half a loaf is better than none

There are times when a draw is very useful; achieving a draw against a powerful opponent has been known to win a great master tournament. That's what happened, for example, in the Semmering Tournament of 1926, one of the greatest master tournaments ever held. In the last round Spielmann, who was leading the tournament half a point ahead of Alekhine, was paired with his leading rival.

Alekhine tried his darnedest to knock Spielmann out of first place. But Spielmann defended doggedly, and at last Alekhine had to concede the draw, leaving Spielmann a clear first! If Spielmann had followed his natural inclination, and played to win, he might well have lost the game and with it the first prize.

In somewhat similar circumstances Pillsbury once played a draw that is reckoned among his finest masterpieces. And, as sporting interest is concerned, the game far surpasses many a routine win. Here is the game:

Halprin – Pillsbury
Ruy Lopez
Munich 1900

1.e4 e5 2.♘f3 ♘c6 3.♗b5 ♘f6

The Berlin Defense was for years Pillsbury's favorite line against the Ruy Lopez. And thereby hangs a tale.

4.0-0 ♘xe4 5.d4 ♘d6

The usual line is now 6.♗xc6 bxc6 7.dxe5 etc. Maroczy and Schlechter, who were running neck and neck with Pillsbury for first place in this tournament, were well aware of his fondness for this defense. They therefore primed Halprin, a tail-ender, with some top-secret analysis that Pillsbury had never seen. They hoped that, when he was confronted with a series of highly original and confusing moves, he would crack under the strain. What actually happened was that Pillsbury found, *over the board*, a superb sequence of moves which had been completely analyzed by his rivals! Imagine how mystified they were by his escape from disaster.

6.d×e5!?

The first surprise. The sacrifice of the piece is only temporary but nevertheless upsetting as an indication that White is playing with borrowed brains.

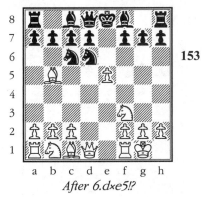
After 6.d×e5!?

6...⌍×b5 7.a4 d6 8.e6!? f×e6 9.a×b5 ⌍e7 10.⌍c3 ⌍g6 11.⌍g5

White must rush the attack before Black has had time to consolidate his position by castling.

11...⌒e7 12.⌕h5 ⌒×g5 13.⌒×g5 ⌔d7

Now White plans to bring his queen rook into the attack via a3. But first he prepares for this by a subtle maneuver.

White of course is playing from memory and consequently produces sensational moves without the slightest exertion.

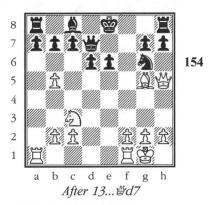
After 13...⌔d7

14.b6!! c×b6 15.⌍d5!!

With the double threat of 16.⌍×b6 or 16.⌍e7. Thus Black must capture the knight, come what may.

15...e×d5 16.⌒fe1+

White loses no time getting to work on the open e-file. After 16...⌔f7 17.⌒e7+ ⌕×e7 18.⌒×e7 ⌔×e7 Black would have an academic plus in material, but his king would be grievously exposed and his position undeveloped.

Pillsbury therefore chooses a course which looks even more hazardous.

16...⌔f8! 17.⌒a3!

White has a devilish threat: 18.⌒f3+ ⌔g8 19.⌒e7! ⌕c6 20.⌒f8+! ⌔×f8 21.⌕f3+ and White mates in three more moves.

The game has now reached its critical stage. Black's game is undeveloped, his king is exposed to the attack of White's

119

aggressive forces. Yet Pillsbury keeps his wits about him and escapes unharmed.

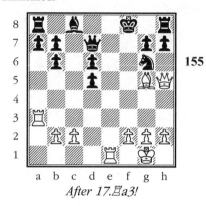

After 17.Ra3!

17...Ne5! 18.Rxe5! dxe5 19.Rf3+ Kg8

At last Pillsbury seems to have achieved a safe position, and he's a whole rook ahead. But White's excellent memory provides a new resource:

20.Bh6!!

After this unexpected move the attack blazes up with new fury, and it requires all of Pillsbury's ingenuity and determination to hold the game together.

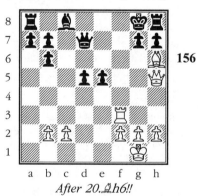

After 20.Bh6!!

Capturing the bishop loses for Black: 20...gxh6 21.Rg3+ Kf8 22.Qxe5 Rg8 23.Qf6+! Kf7 24.Qd8+ etc. Nor would 20...Qe6 do because of 21.Qg5! Qd7 22.Bxg7! when 22...Qxg7 leads to mate after 23.Qd8+.

20...Qe7!

At first sight Black seems helpless against 21.Rg3, for if 21...g6? 22.Rxg6+! wins.

However, on 21.Rg3 Black simply plays 21...Be6!. Then after 22.Rxg7+ Qxg7 23.Bxg7 Kxg7 he has an easy win because of his plus material.

But now we see the final point of the prepared analysis:

21.Bxg7!

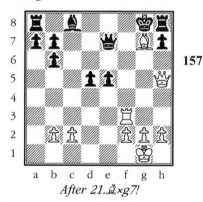

After 21.Bxg7!

Black must watch his step, for after 21...Qxg7?? 22.Qe8+ it is mate next move.

And if 21...Bd7 22.Bxh8 Kxh8 23.Rf7 winning the queen.

21...Kxg7!

This is possible because Pillsbury's 20...♕e7! now rules out 21.♕g5#.

22.♖g3+ ♔f8 23.♖f3+ ♔g7 24.♖g3+ ♔f8 Drawn

No wonder this thrilling game has been called "the most beautiful tournament draw."

And admit it. Have you ever played over many more thrilling or exciting games? Draws are all dull? Rubbish!

Another preconceived notion you have is this:

A bishop is better than a knight

Too many chess writers have made this dogmatic assertion without realizing that the average player is incapable of demonstrating this superiority.

Not only that, but the so-called superiority has been greatly exaggerated. Consequently, you're often misled into playing for this superiority, which may be only imaginary, when you'd be much better off spending your time making sure none of your pieces are attacked.

Furthermore, you may be totally unprepared for the shocking discovery that in some positions it's the knight that's superior! Here's a case in point:

Reinfeld – Fine
New York 1930

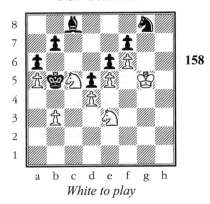

158

White to play

At first sight Black seems to have the edge, as he has a bishop against a knight, and he's on the point of winning a pawn.

Actually Black is dead lost! In positions where the bishop is hemmed in by its own pawns, the bishop has very little scope. In the diagrammed position, as a matter of fact, the bishop cannot move at all.

The pawn position, too, is much against Black. Note his f-pawn, which is highly vulnerable. If White can capture this weak pawn, he will soon queen his own far-advanced f-pawn. This supplies the key to White's procedure:

1.♘g4!

White is about to remove Black's f-pawn. Black is powerless to stop him.

1...♔xa5 2.♘h6! ♘xh6 3.♔xh6 ♔b4 4.♔g7

Now White is about to remove the only obstacle to his getting a new queen.

4...b6 5.♘a4 b5 6.♘c5 ♚c3 7.♚×f7 ♚×d4 8.♚g7 Resigns

Black can't prevent the passed pawn from queening. Note that throughout the whole ending Black's bishop was helpless. So much for doctrinaire theory!

Overprotecting the Castled Position

In Chapter 5 I stressed the importance of not weakening the castled position. As you saw in that chapter, moving the pawns in front of your king creates welcome targets for your opponent's attack. However, if you become hard-shelled about this, you're likely to avoid creating a loophole for your king. The result? You may wind up getting mated by an unforeseen queen or rook move on the back rank.

So, in positions where your opponent has no prospects on the kingside, it's a good idea to interpolate some such move as h2-h3 or g2-g3. Once you've made room for your king's escape, you need worry no longer about a surprise mate.

In Diagram 159 you can see how lurking danger on the back rank may lead to disaster.

White's knight is under attack. Should he capture the c-pawn, or should he retreat his knight to d4?

None of Black's pieces menace the kingside. Consequently White should have made a loophole earlier for his king by moving one of the paws in front of the castled king. h2-h3, for instance, would have been the way.

That's what White should have done. If he had, he could now safely play ♘×c3.

But the fact is that White neglected the precaution. Therefore he must not play ♘×c3, and instead he must content himself with ♘d4.

In the actual game, White completely missed the point by playing:

1.♘×c3??

This is what happened:

1...♘×c3 2.♖×c3 ♖×c3 3.♖×c3 ♛b2!!

Bernstein – Capablanca
Moscow 1914

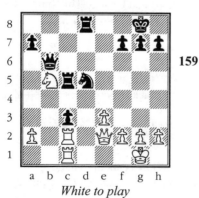

159

White to play

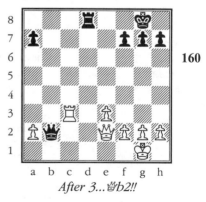

160

After 3...♛b2!!

Black's spectacular queen move has taken cruel advantage of White's inadequately protected first rank.

If White plays 4.♕×b2 Black replies 4...♖d1#. Or if 4.♕e1 ♕×c3! 5.♕×c3 ♖d1+ forcing checkmate. White has other tries, but none of them will do; for example, 4.♖c2 ♕b1+ 5.♕f1 ♕×c2.

So, finding it impossible to stop the mate and also save his rook, White resigned in the position of Diagram 160. Had he played h2-h3 or g2-g3 at an earlier stage, Black's combination could not have worked.

When pawn moves are good

In this book – and in every other chess book you've read – you've been warned not to make too many pawn moves in the opening. Such moves, you've been told time and time again, waste time. They slow down the development of your pieces. They create weaknesses in your position. All very true, every word of it.

But, here too you must discriminate between a useful principle and a useless platitude. Once in a while you arrive at an *exceptional* position when pawn moves are called for. In such a position a whole series of pawn moves may actually be the most forceful line you can adopt.

Marshall, an artful and irreverent player, knew how to handle exceptional positions. Here he punishes Black mercilessly for mistakenly believing that faulty development can serve some useful purpose. So, consider this startling exception:

Marshall – Ragozin
Sicilian Defense
New York 1940

1.e4 c5 2.b4 c×b4 3.a3 ♘c6?

This "developing" move is bad, as the knight will be driven from pillar to post. The right way would be 3...d5! and if 4.e×d5 ♕×d5 as White cannot play 5.♘c3 to drive the queen away.

4.a×b4 ♘f6?

More development – more faulty development, that is.

5.b5 ♘d4? 6.c3 ♘e6 7.e5 ♘d5 8.c4 ♘df4?

This loses a piece! Black had to play 8...♘b6, but even then his position would have been disagreeable.

White's loss of time with the pawn moves is really not as serious as it looks, as Black has also been losing time with his knight moves.

9.g3 ♘g6 10.f4

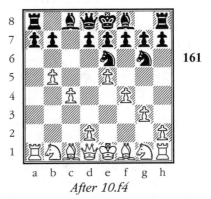

After 10.f4

Black has no defense to the coming f4-f5, for example 10...♘c7 11.f5! ♘×e5 12.d4 winning a piece. Or 10...f5

11.e×f6 and Black is still helpless against the coming f4-f5.

10...♘g×f4 11.g×f4 ♘×f4

Black has three pawns for the piece, but this is not enough in the opening stage. Meanwhile White continues to rely on pawn moves.

12.d4 ♘g6 13.h4

Threatening to win the other knight with h4-h5!.

13...e6 14.h5

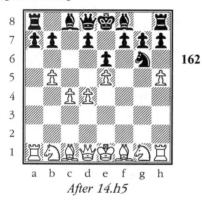

After 14.h5

How is it that White has been able to make 14 consecutive pawn moves without moving a single piece and without coming to grief?

The answer is that Black's so-called "development" was worthless. Consequently White was able to take all sorts of liberties. Nevertheless he deserves great credit for his daring and for his freedom from preconceptions. Most players would have drawn back in horror from such a series of pawn moves.

14...♗b4+ 15.♗d2 ♗×d2+ 16.♘×d2 ♘e7 17.♘e4 ♘f5 18.h6! g6

On 18...♘×h6 19.♘d6+ ♔e7 20.♖×h6 g×h6 21.♕h5 ♕g8 22.♘f3 with a tremendous initiative.

The text is equally unpromising.

19.♘f6+ ♔f8 20.♘f3 d6 21.♘g5! d×e5 22.d×e5 ♕×d1+

Seeking relief – but he doesn't get it. For White's pressure is so powerful that the disappearance of the queens does not diminish it.

23.♖×d1 ♔e7 24.♖h3 b6 25.♗g2 ♖b8 26.♘g×h7 Resigns

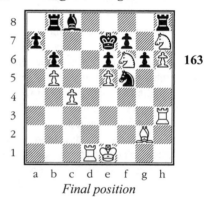

Final position

White threatens checkmate by 27.♖hd3 and 28.♖d7+. Hence 26...♖d8 is inevitable. But then comes 27.♖×d8 ♔×d8 28.♘f8 followed by the advance and queening of the h-pawn. Thus White relied on pawns right to the very end of this unconventional game.

I could multiply these examples indefinitely. But I think I've made my point. It's not enough for you to understand general principles; you must also understand the exceptions that alter cases.

When you come right down to it, all the various reasons why you lose at chess can be summed up in one dictum: you play mechanically and thoughtlessly. You plod along in the same old groove. How can you change – and change, of course, for the better?

My first advice to you is: Know thyself! Know what kind of chess player you are. Know what type of game best suits you.

Once you understand your temperament and your chess style, head for the kind of game in which you're at your best. Avoid the kind of game in which you're weak. Only then can you cultivate your good points and eliminate the bad features of your play.

As you analyze your own style, you'll inevitably get a new slant on the play of your opponents. Play to their weakness. "Hit 'em where they ain't" is just as good tactics in chess as on the baseball diamond.

You lose because you play the openings without thinking. Either you play blindly, making one meaningless move after another, or you go through the motions of following some famous authority.

To lick the first of these difficulties, you must play with some plan. It needn't be fancy. Just remember that what you do at the start will determine your future. Set yourself some simple goal, even if it's nothing more elaborate than bringing out some pieces and getting ready to castle.

By following such a plan, you'll find that you're no longer spoiling your opening *and the whole game as well*. Stop fighting with one hand tied behind your back. Give yourself a fair fighting chance of success.

How can you overcome the second difficulty of opening play – that of following some famous authority? You know what happens when you rely on brand names. As soon as your opponent veers away from the book, you're at a loss. Just when you need your guide most, his usefulness abruptly ends. Granted, the psychological defect on you is very bad.

Your own common sense will help you here. As long as you rely on the books, you'll always be thrown off your stride by moves never seen before on land or sea. Again, the answer to your problem is to devote a minimum of simple planning to the opening. You'll gain skill and confidence, and you'll avoid getting into a mess from which you can't recover.

One of the valuable guides to playing the opening with your own ideas is to observe the importance of the center. You lose many a game because you bypass this all-important principle. Remember this basic rule: the stronger your control of the center, the better your prospects are.

Right here you have the solution to one of your most worrisome problems. If your opponent, through craftiness or ignorance, plays an unusual opening, you immediately panic. But, from now on, instead of reacting instinctively, suppose you just look this unusual opening in the eye. You will learn some curious and interesting things about it.

All openings are a struggle for the center. If an opening is unusual, it has that status because it cedes the other side a monopoly of the center. An unusual opening simply doesn't offer a struggle for control of the center.

So there's your cue. Instead of reacting fearfully against an unusual opening, you can proceed with the greatest confidence. Control the center, and victory is yours.

You lose because you're too impressed by stories about great masters who see 18 moves deep with many parenthetical subvariations. Take these stories with a grain of salt. There's nothing more maddening than missing what's right under your nose because you're daydreaming about some long-range plan. While you're dallying with one of these impressive-looking projects, your opponent may checkmate you on the move. Such things have happened.

Here's what to do: look for the simple, powerful, violent moves. Don't overlook checks or gains of material. Don't set you sights too far ahead; if you do, you'll be confused by all the manifold possibilities.

Look for forceful moves with clear-cut consequences. In that way you'll create order out of chaos. Look for the obvious, decisive moves – they're there! – and you'll convert many a present loss into a future win.

You lose, too, because you like to attack. Who doesn't? The will to win is not enough. You need better qualifications, such as this knowledge:

Do you possess the winning factors of attack? Are they present in this case? If they are, you can win. If they're not, you should lose. It's as simple as that.

But remember this: if you attack *merely* because you feel like it, that's not chess. It's gambling. You might just as well base your attack on what the tea leaves say. It'll do you just about as much good!

You lose because the endgame bores you stiff. Just like your prejudice in favor of attack, your prejudice against endgames hurts your play immensely. So what happens? You're constantly giving odds to the other fellow – and what odds! Remember that 60 per cent of all games are decided in the ending stage.

Just the sheer mathematics of it makes it absolutely essential for you to become interested in the endgame. But, in addition, such an interest will give your play a deep and mature quality. If your opponent thinks he can gain an advantage by steering the game into an ending, you can go right along, serene in the knowledge that you're not being hounded into a type of chess that you loathe.

In short: the better you like the endgame, the more games you'll win.

You lose because you play the board and not the man. You lose, that is, because you don't know the difference between one player and another. It's all one to you whether you're playing Sammy Reshevsky or Joe Palooka. All you do is play the board. How do you know that what won't work against Sammy won't work against Joe as well?

Learn to differentiate among your opponents. You'll find out soon enough that the kind of play that's all wrong against A works fine against B, and so on. If you ask me, "Should I play the King's Gambit?" I'd answer you with a question: "Play it against whom?" A simple yes-or-no answer would be a foolish one.

You lose because you're lazy. You think that having a hobby means "taking it easy." Actually, you'll find that the people who get the most pleasure out of their hobbies are the ones who devote the most effort to them.

If you want to win, you must make an effort to get rid of your playing weaknesses. Neglect that effort, and your losing streak will go on.

And you lose because you're stuck in the mud. You're inflexible. You won't change. As I've just been saying, the only way to improve – to stop losing at chess – is to change your losing ways.

As matters stand, you lose because you continue to take things for granted. You lose because you fail to take advantage of the short-cut techniques that enable you to play a foolproof attack – or to plan a winning endgame.

You lose, in short, because you lack the expert knowledge of what to do, and when to do it.

Cheer up! There are factors in your favor too. Books and study are never the complete answer to improving your game. Look at Grünfeld, that walking encyclopedia of the openings. He knew more about the openings than any master of his time, yet that never put him in the front rank. The moral is: read the books, sure, but don't be enslaved by them.

Remember, too, that chess is more than applying general principles and memorizing specific techniques. It's a struggle between two human beings. That's why psychology – sizing up your opponent – is often more important than technical playing skill. Ignore those psychological factors and you'll continue behind the eight ball.

Don't despair too readily; don't give up hope too easily. In chess, the race is not always to the swift, nor the battle to the strong. Be more confident, more self-reliant. As you plunge into problems which look hopeless to you, you'll find out that in chess certain skills are much easier to acquire than you think they are. But don't sell yourself short! Don't start with the thought: "Oh, I can never learn to play these damn endings!" Try them, and you'll find they're not as hard, or as unrewarding, as you think.

So again I say, have confidence. It's an asset, perhaps the greatest. But it's not an asset that can be weighed or measured. It's not something you can get from books. But once you have it, it improves your play so enormously that you will hardly recognize yourself as the fellow who *used* to lose at chess.

Chess, I've often heard tell, is a lot of fun. And I always answer "Yes, chess is a lot of fun, but it's a lot more fun when you win."

I shall never forget the description of the final scene of the 1935 match for the world championship. Both Alekhine, the defeated champion, and Euwe, the new champion, were in tears. There was this difference: Alekhine, the defeated, wept tears of sorrow. Euwe, the victor, wept tears of joy.

So you're not a world champion. Still, it means a lot to you whether you win or lose. You want to win; but you lose consistently. It is my contention that you lose 50 per cent more games than you should – not through any lack of technical skill, but because you are unaware of, and ignore, the psychological factors which enter into and control the most cruelly competitive of all contests: a game of chess.

Notes from the Editor

Page 36 – Many other moves also allow mate, e.g., 7.♘c3, 7.♘g3, etc..

Page 44 – 1...c5 is not only not prevented, it is also Black's best move, striking at White's strong center.

Page 116 – Not really – Black wins with ease by exchanging the heavy pieces with check and marching the h-pawn.